Twayne's English Authors Series

EDITOR OF THIS VOLUME

Herbert Sussman

Northeastern University

T. E. Brown

TEAS 213

T. E. Brown

T. E. BROWN

By RICHARD C. TOBIAS

University of Pittsburgh

TWAYNE PUBLISHERS
A DIVISION OF G. K. HALL & CO., BOSTON

Published in 1978 by Twayne Publishers,
A Division of G. K. Hall & Co.
All Rights Reserved

Printed on permanent/durable acid-free paper and bound
in the United States of America

First Printing

Library of Congress Cataloging in Publication Data

Tobias, Richard Clark, 1925–
T. E. Brown.

(Twayne's English authors series ; TEAS 213)
Bibliography: p. 177–181
Includes index.
1.   Brown, Thomas Edward, 1830–1897—Criticism and
interpretation.
PR4175.B5T6   821'.8   78–7818
ISBN 0–8057–6682–0

For Leslie

Contents

About the Author

Richard Tobias edits the annual "Victorian Bibliography" appearing each June in the journal *Victorian Studies.* During the ten-year period 1963–1972, he wrote "The Year's Work in Victorian Poetry," an annual world-wide survey of scholarship, for the journal *Victorian Poetry,* and he continues to contribute to the annual "Guide to the Year's Work in Victorian Poetry." He has published articles in *Philological Quarterly, Modern Philology,* and *Victorian Studies.*

In 1975 and 1978, Mr. Tobias chaired the Executive Committee of the Victorian Division, Modern Language Association. From 1971 to 1975 he served in the Delegate Assembly of the Modern Language Association.

In 1970, Ohio University Press published his book, *The Art of James Thurber.* He has edited for the same press, *Shakespeare's Late Plays,* a collection of humanistic essays on Shakespeare's last four plays.

Mr. Tobias was born in Xenia, Ohio, and he has taught at The Ohio State University, the University of Colorado, and, since 1957, at the University of Pittsburgh.

In 1965 and 1970, Mr. Tobias visited the Isle of Man to collect materials for his biography of T. E. Brown. Although he has no Manx ancestors, he considers himself Manx by election and fascination.

Preface

This book started as a straightforward study of Thomas Edward Brown, a Manxman whose poems, letters, and biography were until 1970 in print.[1] His poems, however, were not published as he wrote them. His letters were rewritten, cut, or unpublished. The previous biography, a "Memoir" signed by Sir Arthur Quiller-Couch, was actually written by another man. This book, therefore, reveals a Thomas Edward Brown unknown before.

The Manx Museum Library at Douglas, Isle of Man, holds rare first editions of Brown's poems in Manx dialect. These editions, published on newsprint, are one-seventh longer than the trade edition that Macmillan published in 1881 and the edition that continued in print until the 1970s. Brown preferred his original text, but all criticism is based on later corrupt editions. Although he is the national poet of the Isle of Man, Manxmen know only these bowdlerized texts.

The Manx Museum also holds original manuscripts of Brown's letters, but they too differ greatly from the text in the often-reprinted volume of letters. Published versions omit references to family feuds, drinking parties, and monetary troubles. In addition, the Museum has letters — including an astonishing defense of Brown's own orthodoxy — that have never been published.

Readers of the "Memoir" in *Thomas Edward Brown: A Memorial Volume,* signed by Sir Arthur Quiller-Couch, may admire the way "Q" (as he was known) captured the Manx landscape. The Introduction by Ramsey Moore thanks William Radcliffe for gathering biographical material.[2] Only readers of Manx newspapers could know how much thanks Radcliffe deserved, for Radcliffe's own text ran serially in the Ramsey *Courier* in May and June, 1930, the same spring the *Memorial Volume* appeared.[3] Radcliffe was a Manxman who knew the landscape well. The text is almost identical. "Q," in his version, adds a paragraph or two, changes words here and there, and rearranges some of the material. On page 38, "Q" writes, "I, who edit this Memoir, may here interpose a personal anecdote," but how many readers would notice what, if done by a student or a professional writer, law courts might call plagiarism?

The basic facts of Brown's life are unremarkable. He was born in 1830 on the Isle of Man, an island in the Irish Sea halfway between Liverpool and Belfast. He was an undergraduate at Christ Church, Oxford (1849-53), and a fellow at Oriel College (1854-55). During most of his adult life (1864-1892), he taught at a secondary school, Clifton College, in suburban Bristol. He published five books of verse; about eighty percent of his writing is in the modern Manx dialect, a variation of English Midlands dialect not difficult to read. The other twenty percent is written in standard English.

Brown was, however, living a dual life. He wrote to a friend who was worrying about his prospects of life as a schoolmaster, "My plan always was to recognize two lives as necessary — the one the outer kapelistic life of drudgery, the other the inner and cherished life of the spirit. It is true that the one has a tendency to kill the other, but it must not, and you must see that it does not."[4]

Brown lived the outward drudgery of a successful teacher at a great nineteenth-century middle-class school. His real life was inner. His first national publication, "Christ Church Servitors in 1852: By One of Them," in the November, 1868, issue of *Macmillan's Magazine,* attacked his Oxford college for systematic persecution of its poor but struggling scholarship students, called Servitors. The essay was signed "BETA," an inversion of the initials T.E.B. that Brown always used as his signature. At Oxford, Servitors lived in secluded quarters, ate forty-five minutes after other members of the college, and even sat in special seats at divine service. Brown's Oxford sheds no enchantments of the Middle Ages as Matthew Arnold's Oxford did (although they were near contemporaries); Brown seemed deliberately to contradict James Anthony Froude's bumptious enthusiasms in his "Words About Oxford" (published in 1850 under the nom de plume "Zeta").[5] For reasons which this study will explore, Brown's poetry had its beginnings in his essay on Oxford, as if stating the pain of his experience had opened a sluice in his emotional life. Oxford trained him to live "two lives," but stubbornly TEB did not let Oxford or England kill his inner, cherished life of the spirit. Behind the public demeanor walked a very different man.

The real TEB is fit to be the hero of a Russian novel or an English biography. He entangled himself desperately in the intellectual, artistic, and sexual problems of his time. His father, after what was probably a nervous breakdown, died in terrible circumstances, leaving his family destitute. TEB gave over his Oriel fellowship in order to marry a woman so painfully shy that she could not participate in academic social life. TEB's hope to serve in the Manx Church as God's priest was frustrated because Oxford — still in the throes of the High Church Movement — made Brown unfit to serve the Low Church, Evangelical Manx Bishops. His best friend said, "the less said about his life as a clergyman, the better."[6] His one chance to advance his educational career he threw away by an ill-timed and ill-tempered letter to a Gloucester newspaper. The young poets and writers at Clifton College, among whom were Quiller-Couch and Sir Henry Newbolt, did not know Brown; Brown taught on the Modern Side rather than the Classical Side where the young intellectuals were all at play. When TEB retired to the Isle of Man, he became an entertainer, a raconteur, a Manx Uncle Tom. His poems had a small audience because he insisted on writing in dialect. The Manx suspect he laughs at them; the English ignore him.

The story of his literary reputation reads equally like a black comedy. Brown himself disavowed the text of his poems that Macmillan printed. Brown wrote the lively, immediate language of his fellow Manx; Macmillan tried to remake the text into a drawing room book about charming Celts. Anthologists unerringly select his worst poems. His best poems, in fairness, are too long to be included in typical compendia. One poem, "My Garden," passed directly from Quiller-Couch's *Oxford Book of English Verse* (it was the final poem) to *The Stuffed Owl: An Anthology of Bad Verse*. The editors of *The Stuffed Owl* had superior taste. It is a bad poem, but Brown wrote it for a very special audience, for which his tone was appropriate. Because Brown knew William Ernest Henley and Sir Henry Newbolt, he could be bracketed with a school called the Victorian Activists, a group of writers who attempted muscular Romanticism in opposition to the Decadents around Oscar Wilde.[7] Brown did attempt a return to the direct language of William Wordsworth, but his healthy men and women hold somber and desperate views that contradict both the Activists and the Decadents of the 1880s and 1890s. Moreover, Brown was humorous. Since he began writing in the 1860s and 1870s, he belongs more properly with Matthew Arnold, Arthur Hugh Clough, and William Morris than with the poets at the end of the century. Brown's interest in the

Celt had nothing to do with the Celtic Twilight. William Butler Yeats never refers to TEB (Yeats's father went to school on the Isle of Man), but Yeats would have wanted a more elegant, mystical, and dreamy view of the Celt. Brown's Celts were deeply involved in their present and Brown dreamed no airy future for them. TEB is an anomaly, difficult to categorize and therefore easy to ignore.

Late in Brown's life, a friend reported in dismay that Brown had been omitted from a list of minor writers of the Victorian period. Brown smiled and said, "Perhaps I am among the major."[8] Fortunately Brown had sufficient irony in him to justify such a remark. As a Manx poet, Brown was major. Far superior to all others who have written about the island, he is recognized as the national poet of the Isle of Man. As a dialect poet, he ranks with Robert Burns although his method differs greatly from Burns's. He ranks above James Russell Lowell and William Barnes; Brown's dialect verse displays more intelligence and a larger canvas. His twelve Manx narratives are, in effect, an epic of modern Manx life as well as a dramatization of the conflict with English culture. In his bones he knew that English culture would annihilate the culture of his Manx sailors, farmers, and innocent women, but although Brown knew the sick disease of modern life, his Manx men and women are not yet infected by it.

The world is full of minor ethnic cultures striving to retain integrity and vision against the encroaching molten mass of efficient conformity. The real TEB wrote a dialect epic that deserves reading because it grasps and retains in the amber of art a passing life. Brown's Manx, courageous in their defeat, have character. This study is written to persuade a dominant culture to attend to a major artist of a minor ethnic group. At their remote edge of the world, Brown's Manx live warm and satisfying lives that enrich our lives.

Acknowledgments

Many Manxmen have helped me to understand TEB and the Isle of Man. A farmer, one squally Sunday afternoon, guided me down a public path which Brown had lobbyed to establish. The Director of the Manx Museum and National Trust Library, A.M. Cubbon, shared with me his deep knowledge of Manx life. The Archivist, Ann Harrison, answered questions, arranged to have microfilm made, helped to decipher manuscripts, and introduced me to other Manxmen. The assistant librarian, Ms. J. Narashimhan, pointed out the unknown biography of TEB. The Library and the Museum provided pleasant facilities for work.

Through Ann Harrison, I met Ramsey B. Moore in April, 1965. He was the only Manxman yet alive who knew Brown. Mr. Moore, formerly Attorney-General of the Isle of Man, descends from a distinguished Manx family. Ramsey Moore died in 1968. Another friend, J.B. Caine, loaned me his valuable Manx books, took me to dinner, and guided me around the island. He read an early version of this manuscript. Alan Cooper showed me modern Manx life.

Simon Nowell-Smith of the London Library sent me his *Book Collector* essay which I have used constantly. Dr. James B. Russell of Glasgow, guided me with his infinite energy and inquiring mind. My wife bore separation, work, and my errors with fortitude.

The unpublished letters quoted in this work are in the Manx Museum and National Trust library. The Librarian of the Gloucester City Libraries found the public documents of Brown's life in Gloucester. The staff of the British Museum Library (now called the British Library) and the University of Pittsburgh Hillman Library proved that librarianship is a noble profession.

A grant from the Council on International Studies, University of Pittsburgh, enabled me to spend two months working on the Isle of Man and in England.

The following have granted permission to quote copyrighted materials:

Liverpool University Press for permission to quote from the

Letters of T.E. Brown (ed. S. Irwin) and the *Poems of T.E. Brown;*
Cambridge University Press for permission to quote from
Thomas Edward Brown: A Memorial Volume, 1830–1930;

Macmillan, London and Basingstoke, for permission to quote
from *Letters to Macmillan*, edited by Simon Nowell-Smith.

Barbara Tobias prepared the index.

Chronology

1830 Thomas Edward Brown born May 5, New Bond Street, Douglas, Isle of Man.

1832 Family moves to Vicarage, Kirk Braddan.

1846 TEB enters King William's College, Castletown, Isle of Man.

1847 Wins second prize at King William's for poem (Dean Farrar wins first).

1849 March, leaves King William's; October 17, matriculates at Oxford; Awarded Servitorship at Christ Church.

1850 January, residence at Oxford; November, wins Boulter Scholarship.

1853 Double First at Oxford.

1854 April 21, elected Fellow, Oriel College.

1855 January, publishes anonymously at Oxford (in collaboration with Henry Earle Tweed) *The Student's Guide to the School of "Litterae Fictitae;"* May, appointed Vice-Principal, King William's College; ordained by Samuel Wilberforce, Bishop of Oxford.

1857 June 24, marries Amelia Stowell, Kirk Maughold, Isle of Man.

1861 Spring, appointed Headmaster, Crypt School, Gloucester; August 1, Crypt school reopens under new statutes; August 6, letter signed "Paterfamilias" in *Gloucestershire Chronicle*; August 10, TEB's answer published; William Ernest Henley admitted to Crypt School.

1863 August 19, TEB resigns as Headmaster, Crypt School. October 15, ends teaching duties.

1864 Master, Modern Side, Clifton College, Bristol.

1868 June 8–November 27, writes 18 lyric poems; November, *Macmillan* essay on Christ Church published.

1872 "Betsy Lee" published, Cockermouth, Lake District.

1873 April 5–July 26, "Betsy Lee," in Isle of Man *Times*; April, May, "Betsy Lee," *Macmillan's*; Macmillan trade edition of

"Betsy Lee;" "Christmas Rose" privately printed, Cocker-mouth; December 7, completes mss. of "Captain Tom and Captain Hugh."

1874   Writing "The Doctor."

1875   March 7, mother dies (born 1796); poems in *Plain Talk,* parish magazine of Myrtle Street Baptist Church, Liverpool; "Chalse a Killey" published.

1876   "The Doctor" published, Isle of Man *Times;* November, Preface to "Captain Tom and Captain Hugh;" November 25, "Mary Quayle" in manuscript; December 15–January 12, 1878, "Captain Tom and Captain Hugh," in Isle of Man *Times.*

1879   November-April, 1880, "Tommy Big Eyes," in Isle of Man *Times.*

1880   June, completes "Bella Gorry."

1881   *Fo'c's'le Yarns* published by Macmillan.

1884   Licensed by Bishop of Gloucester as curate of St. Barnabas, Bristol (Clifton College Mission Church).

1887   *The Doctor and Other Poems* published by Swan Sonnen-schein.

1888   February 7, Amelia ill. July 3, Amelia dies.

1889   Macmillan reprints *Fo'c's'le Yarns; The Manx Witch and Other Poems* published by Macmillan.

1891   TEB seriously ill.

1892   July 2, retires from Clifton College; moves to Isle of Man.

1893   *Old John and Other Poems* published by Macmillan.

1895   "Job the White" in *New Review* (last Manx narrative).

1896   "Prologue: Spes Altera, To the Future Manx Poet."

1897   October 1, leaves Isle of Man for visit to Clifton College; October 29, dies, Tait's House, Clifton College.

1900   *Collected Poems. Letters.*

CHAPTER 1

Anchises, or a Wordsworth Letter: Before 1830

> Deep in a valley of green, father Anchises
> Was watching,
> . . .
> All his race to come, his dear descendants,
> . . .
> And as he saw Aeneas coming toward him
> Over the meadow, his hands reached out with
> yearning,
> He was moved to tears, and called: — "At last, my
> son, —
> Have you really come, at last?"
> . . .
> And his son answered: — "It was your spirit, father,
> Your sorrowful shade, so often met, that led me
> To find these portals. . . .
> Embrace me, father;
> Let hand join hand in love; do not forsake me."
>
> *The Aeneid of Virgil*[1]

THOMAS Edward Brown carried his past just as Aeneas carried his father Anchises from burning Troy. Four years before TEB's birth, his father, Robert Brown, published a poem, "My Native Land," an earnest call for a genuine Manx poet. Near the end of his life TEB repeated the call in his "The Future Manx Poet." TEB was answering his father's spirit; in his Manx narratives TEB was his own Aeneas and his own Virgil.

Both men looked for their Rome in that lozenge-shaped island homeland in the middle of the Irish Sea between Liverpool and Belfast. Further, both wrote in the nineteenth century, a time when cultural events made men conscious that they differed (to use the

17

formula of Taine, the French historian of English literature) because of *race, moment, et milieu*. They sought to know their people, to distinguish their time from others, and to taste, smell, and see their world. In the eighteenth century a poet hid his individual traits, preferring the *consensus gentium*. Robert Brown wrote in eighteenth-century English; all the words in "My Native Land," his poem about a future Aeneas who would "really come, at last," are in Dr. Johnson's *Dictionary*. In the nineteenth century, Wordsworth taught poets to use words "uttered by men in real life."[2] Wordsworth saw Robert Brown's poem, approved its sentiments, and praised it for its "naturalness." Robert Brown, like Anchises, thus led his son Thomas Edward Brown "to find [those] portals" and explain the meaning of being a Manxman in the nineteenth century.

I   *Isle of Man*

Even Englishmen may be excused for having forgotten that geographical, historical, and constitutional anomaly off the coast of Cumberland. Outsiders may know that the tailless Manx cat is native to the island. Americans may remember a mysterious Manxman in Herman Melville's *Moby Dick*. Motorcyclists know the Tourist Trophy Race each June, the premier race for motorcycles in the world. Outsiders do not connect the word *Manx* with the word *Man*. Americans confuse the Isle of Man with the Isle of Wight (off Britain's southern coast). The Romans also could never quite get the name straight. They called the island *Mona*, but the name was applied to the present-day Isle of Man and also to the Isle of Anglesey off the coast of Wales. Undigested bits at the far outposts of empire still remain undigested.

The name has nothing to do with the English word *man*. It may have more to do with the Highland Gaelic *monadh*, the Welsh *mynydd*, the Latin *mons*,[3] or the Irish *mana*.[4] These are all words for *mountain* and since Snaefell (Norse: snow mountain) rises to two thousand feet and two-thirds of the island is mountainous, the word is accurate and proper. Celtic studies produce a more romantic explanation. A ninth-century glossary records that "Mannin McLir was a celebrated merchant who lived in the Isle of Man. He was the most famous pilot of western Europe. He used to know, by studying the heavens, the period of fine and bad weather, and of their change one to another."[5] The unstable weather around the island suggests that McLir deserved his celebration. The fourteenth-century *Book of Fermoy* goes a step further; it mentions a Mannanan, "a pagan necromancer who possessed the ability to envelop himself and his island in a mist, to make them invisible to strangers and enemies."[6] Another version of his name is Manna Beg-Mac-y-Leirr, translated as Little Mannanan, Son of the Sea;[7] and moving that name just a step along the way of the human mind, the island seems to be named for the Celtic Neptune or Poseidon, god of the sea. When the head of the Manx Church is denominated "Bishop of Sodor and Man," his title includes another empire's name for its outpost. After the Norse invasion in the ninth century, two petty Norse kingdoms developed in the islands off the Scottish coast: to the north the Nordreys, including Shetland and the Orkneys, and to the south the *Sudreyjar* or Sudreys (Latin Sodorensis, modern Sodor),[8] including Man, Lewes, Skye, and others. Thus the Bishop's title joins the Latin form of a Norse word for *south* to an Indo-European root word for *mountain.*

Even though the Isle of Man is almost in the geographical center of the British Isles, the island itself was at the periphery of empire. The Romans stopped at the English shore. Irish Christianity arrived in 447, but it died when the Norse began raiding and plundering and finally settling. The Norse Kingdom of Man was the southernmost extremity of direct rule; its bishops were first consecrated at Trondheim, but some of them never made the long journey for the festivity and one died on the way home. The Norse kings probably became independent because no one could venture so far to say "no" to them. During the dark period of Manx history, between 1266 and 1405, when England and Scotland fought over the island, it was very remote from both Edinburgh and London. Today the island rules itself, largely ignored by prime ministers and the daily newspapers.

Manx history falls into five major periods: (1) pre-history up to and including the time of Celtic Christianity which came to the island in 447, (2) the Norse incursions from 800 to 1266, (3) the period between 1266 and 1405 when the island was the football of English and Scottish noblemen, (4) the rule of the Stanley family from 1405 to 1765 (they are known better as the English Earls of Derby and Dukes of Atholl), and (5) the constitutional period from 1765 to the present, when the reigning monarch of England holds the title Lord of Man. Bits of pottery, some grave sites, over two hundred keills (cells or oratories established by Irish monks), and remnants of the Manx language survive from that first period. Manxmen today insist that they are Celts in the blood and marrow, but the language is gone except in family and place names and except for hardy souls who teach it to themselves. Huge stone crosses from the Norse period show fragments of runic script and legendary actors from the *Nibelunglied*. The government, parish boundaries, and land-tenure system also derive from the Scandinavians. After seven hundred years, the Manx have accepted (or had forced on them) the language of the English. T. E. Brown, their national poet, knew only phrases and snatches of Manx; he wrote in English, albeit a dialect form used on the island.

The astonishing fact of this history is its silence. A phrase remains on a runic stone; an ancient visitor reports impoverished island dwellers. The Manx have some modern legends, but of their past they know only legends of King Gorry, a Norse king whose story is mingled with events from Irish history. The only Manx literary form is the "carvels" or carols, but the form is minor and late. Since 1830 (the year of TEB's birth) the Isle of Man Steam Packet Company has brought daily summer invaders, tourists from the English Midlands.

II   *Poetry of Robert Brown*

Thus Robert Brown's book of poems is especially interesting. It is probably the first book published in London by a Manxman who was willing to put the fact of his origin on the title page. Bishop Wilson, a Manx divine celebrated by Matthew Arnold, had published books, but Bishop Wilson was not native and few of his readers knew or cared about his See. Robert Brown's *Poems: Principally On Sacred Subjects* was published in 1826.[9] The book belongs to an eighteenth-century cultural phenomenon, the work of poor but worthy men who have learned to speak the language of polite society. In America, Phillis Wheatley, a Negro slave educated in Massachusetts, learned to write couplets; in England, Stephen Duck did the same. The main interest is, as Dr. Johnson commented on women preaching or dogs walking on their hind legs, not so much in the poems as in the fact that they occur.

Robert Brown's book is thoroughly an example of Evangelical piety and eighteenth-century language decorum. One poem, its diction still in the old pattern, gropes toward new consciousness; "My Native Land" seems to come from a valley of green, like that where

Anchises saw his son Aeneas, and in the poem Brown (as Anchises) yearns for an "immortal bard" who will sing about his native land:

Island of Mountains steep and bare!
Bleak is thy climate, and thy soil
But ill repays the planter's care,
But ill rewards the reaper's toil:
No costly harvests wave on thee,
On thee no forests wide expand;
Yet, Mona, thou hast charms for me,
For art not thou my native land?

No rivers deep and broad hast thou,
Like those which flow through British ground;
Thine are but streams, that, from the brow
Of lofty mountains, swiftly bound
Through narrow channels to the sea,
Which bursts upon thy murmuring strand;
Yet, Mona, thou hast charms for me,
For art not thou my native land?

No minstrel of immortal fame
Has yet among thy sons been found,
Nor of the country can we name
A single portion classic ground:
No harp has sounded yet in thee,
Struck by a Gray's or Milton's hand;
Yet, Mona, thou hast charms for me,
For art thou not my native land?

Rough is thy coast, and loud the roar
Around thy rocks of ocean's wave;
The tide that rolls upon thy shore
Has often proved the seaman's grave.
But yet my bosom clings to thee;
Yes! it is nature's own demand,
Island! that thou be dear to me,
For art not thou my native land?

The poem is structured on a tiresome rhetorical device of negation. Brown prefers — he had few better models — the generalized language of forest, lofty mountains, and murmuring strands to exact words. The picture in Robert Brown's poem is very gray, but the island indeed was gray to Robert Brown. TEB said that his father knew little of Manx history; he would not have known where the classic ground was or might have been, but he uses the Latin name for the island. His report on the bad climate, poor soil, shallow rivers, and dangerous coast could have been written from a geography book. The poem interests us now, of course, because his own son, with a far different style, sought to become the minstrel of immortal fame. For his son's poems, Robert Brown might have said with Anchises in Hades, "at last, my son, — / Have you really come, at last?"

Robert Brown died when TEB was only sixteen.

III   *A Wordsworth Letter*

Because Robert Brown's book is so rare, the edition must have been small. A copy was sent to William Wordsworth, and the poet replied:

Dear Sir:
    An apology is due to you for not having sooner thanked you for a Vol. of Poems and an obliging letter received through the hands of Mr. Atkinson. I have read the poems and several of them many times, and with much pleasure, both from the manner and the style in which they are composed, and for the unaffected Piety which breathes through them. There is also one piece, My Native Land, not professedly religious with which I was much gratified. The language is good as is the benefaction, and the sentiments are perfectly natural. With many thanks for this mark of your attention I

                                        remain dear Sir
                                        your obliged servant
                                        Wm Wordsworth

Nov 1st 1827
Rydal Mount
    near Ambleside[10]

Sir Arthur Quiller-Couch in his "Memoir" of Brown says that Wordsworth sent the Brown family a copy of the six-volume edition[11] of Wordsworth's *Poems* in return, but the six-volume edition was not published until a decade later.

IV   *Dorothy Wordsworth's Visit*

The actual circumstances may be more interesting than the "Memoir" suggests. In 1826 or 1827 Wordsworth's brother-in-law and sister-in-law (Henry Hutchinson [1769–1839] and Joanna Hutchinson [1780–1843]) moved to Douglas on the Isle of Man.[12]

They had a small income, but with a small income one could live very comfortably on the Isle of Man (in 1830 it was possible to live in one of the best hotels for one pound a week; a workman would earn one pound a month).[13] The Hutchinsons lived on the South Quay, just opposite St. Matthew's Church,[14] the church Robert Brown served. TEB said in a letter to the Isle of Man *Times* on April 25, 1894, that probably through communication with the Manx Hutchinsons, Wordsworth sent his father an edition of his *Poems* with an autograph presentation. Joanna Hutchinson was godmother to TEB's sister, Dora Brown (born in 1827).[15]

At the end of June and during the first half of July, 1828, Dorothy Wordsworth visited the Hutchinsons and William Wordsworth's youngest son, who was also on the island. She kept a memorable and fascinating travel journal. Unexpectedly, Robert Brown steps onto her stage. On Sunday, June 29, 1828, Dorothy went with Joanna to St. Matthew's to hear Brown preaching on a text from Isaiah, "the 'Shadow of a great Rock', etc., applied to our Savior and the Christian dispensation."[16] Of Robert Brown she says that he is "a sensible and feeling, yet monotonous and weak-voiced, reader." Then with that inexplicable ability to find a surprising detail, she notes, "His ironed shoes clank along the aisle — the effect of this very odd." She means that he wore hobnails on his boots. Afterwards she went to the post office and then walked one and a half miles to Kirk Braddan for a second service (she was late, arriving only for the second lesson).

The next day Dorothy and Joanna called on Mr. Brown, and Dorothy reported:

An old staircase in front, kitchen on one side — close situation — all smooth and orderly but sadly decayed and dull. Mrs. Brown rather a pretty woman about 34, with sweet countenance [she was in fact 32]. Told little boy [Robert Brown who was eight or Hugh Stowell Brown who was five] to tell his father, who was in the study — he received us as if much pleased, and has a pleasant look when he speaks — told me my name was very familiar to him, showed us the room where Bishop Wilson used to lodge — a wee place with fireplace in one corner, — dark coloured flock paper, on each window small panes half wood — had not been on good terms with late Bp., therefore could get nothing done that he wished. No repairs, and could not afford to do any himself. Baby very nice and clean [William Brown, 3, or Dora Brown, 1], and no appearance of discomfort. The present Bishop might do something. The people had been well disposed towards him but he was deceived; rashly supposed the Bishop rich

with 7,000 per annum, whereas, stretched to the utmost by late B., not
more than 2000.[17]

Dorothy Wordsworth was describing the house near the harbor in
New Bond Street, Douglas, where TEB was born. The late Bishop,
the Honorable George Murray, was the last appointment to the See
by the Dukes of Atholl (the Atholl family name is Murray). Brown
was thus in conflict with the main power on the island. Granted a
new bishop promised to help him, but in the meantime Dorothy
noticed the family poverty. Surely the poverty, as it grew worse
(remember Anthony Trollope's poverty-stricken Rev. Josiah
Crawley in *The Last Chronicle of Barset*), exacerbated Brown's
nerves as did his many children. Hugh Stowell Brown described the
poverty in brutal detail; aside from Manx dirt, poverty was
Brown's chief memory of life in the household of a clergyman in
the Established Church.[18]

The cleanliness of the house and baby holds more than casual
interest. Dorothy was a great noticer of such matters, but visitors
often complained about Manx dirt. In 1832, a terrible cholera epidemic raged in the port area where the Brown family lived. Others
reported that the walls of the house "stood cheek by jowl with one
of the most noisome resorts that ever graced a city's name."[19] Part
of Brown's income seems to have come from renting storage room
to smugglers.[20] The wretched house and the old Manx church are
now gone; the new church is imitation gothic and a bus depot
stands on the house site.

The following week Dorothy Wordsworth again heard service at
St. Matthew's, and once again at Kirk Braddan, but her mind was
on her walking tour which began the following day. On her return
to Douglas she settled down to evaluate her experience: the trip
confirmed her

previous notion that with proper culture this island might be made even
more beautiful than the Isle of Wight. In many parts the shores are abrupt,
rocky and bold; in others green yet steep, the rocks mostly of a fine dark
hue, which I think much more striking than the white Southern cliffs of
England. The whole island is well watered, some of the streams (considering their short course) are even considerable, and the glens are fine nur-
series for wood. Besides, wherever wood is seen on the high ground it
thrives. The small clefts or glens are innumerable, and the whole country
except the mountains is sprinkled over with houses and huts. The three
towns of Douglas, Ramsey, and Peel [she found Castletown, the capital,

dirty], especially the two latter, are charmingly situated; yet when I think of the noble Bay of Douglas, and the very pleasing valley behind it, it seems almost unjust to prize it less than the other two places.[21]

Her language is detailed and much more vivid than Robert Brown's verse. The pleasing valley is formed by the Dhoo (Manx for *dark*) and the Glass (for *light*) Rivers which join near Kirk Braddan to make the River Douglas and give the town its name. TEB grew up in the valley behind Douglas that Dorothy Wordsworth praised.

In her circumambulation she had walked nearly fifty miles. She was fifty-seven. On the day after she returned to Douglas, she ''rose late.'' The next day was Sunday, but it was so cold that they had to have a fire and she saw only Henry Hutchinson, Wordsworth's son Willy, and Joanna. On Monday, the 14th of July, Robert Brown returned her call:

Mr. Brown called on Monday morning, [and] gave us much pleasure: there is a mild benevolence in his countenance, and his voice is sweet. He wished I could prevail on Mr. Wordsworth to visit the little island — it would be ''a national honour.'' He informed me that 8 scholars were to be taught *gratis,* besides two others for the ministry, that his school time was six hours. Speaking of his labourious life, and congratulating him self on the present time of holiday, he told me that besides his public duty, 3 sermons weekly and prayers 3 times Sunday, once Wednesday, once Friday, the private duty was much more than anyone suspected; he had mostly 20 sick persons on his list to whom he paid weekly, in general, 2 visits.[22]

Brown was telling her of his duties in the Douglas Grammar School, duties in addition to his being minister of St. Matthew's.

V   *Ancestors*

Dorothy Wordsworth pictured a pious Manxman of Evangelical leanings. Born in 1792, he would have been thirty-four at the time of her visit. Except for the accident of birth, he had little claim to Manxness. His father, Robert Brown also, a captain in the Guinea trade, was lost at sea in 1800.[23] The sea captain was one of two children, the other Ann Brown, of a Scotsman. Ann Brown married Thomas Stowell[24] and produced fifteen sons and one daughter. All fifteen sons were vigorous and energetic men who became journalists, parsons, schoolmasters, and surgeons. TEB married a descendant of the family. The sea captain must have been in his forties

when he married Jane Drumgold of an Irish family that had settled
in Douglas sometime in the eighteenth century. Robert Brown, who
became curate of St. Matthew's, was his only child. Not on his
great-grandfather's side does any native Manx blood appear in
TEB's family.

His great-grandmother was thoroughly Manx. The mother of
Captain Brown and Ann Stowell was Jane Cosnahan, daughter of
the Vicar of Kirk Braddan. Her father was the last of three Cosnahans who were Vicars at Kirk Braddan in the eighteenth century,
but Cosnahans had been Manx vicars since the sixteenth century.[25]
The name derives from a Manx word meaning *defender*.[26] The first
clergyman was John Cosnahan, Vicar of Jurby in 1575. In the eighteenth century Jane Cosnahan, daughter of the Vicar of Braddan,
married Robert Brown, the first Brown on the Isle of Man. Thus
TEB's great-grandmother is the first native Manxman in the
family.

Brown's own mother, the woman that Dorothy Wordsworth
described as a "pretty woman" with a "sweet countenance," was
also of a family that emigrated from Scotland to the Isle of Man in
the eighteenth century. The Scotsmen possibly came to the island to
participate in the smuggling trade. Since the Isle of Man had no
tariff of its own, it was legal to ship a load of brandy from France
to Douglas, and then transship it to England. Or, one could easily
sail a small ship from Douglas and land in one of the many coves
and creeks of the west shore of England. To stop this trade the
English Crown began to buy out the Dukes of Atholl in 1765.

In the late 1730s, the first Brown had married the daughter of an
honored Manx family and of the Vicar of Kirk Braddan. In 1832
Robert Brown — coming home, so to speak — became Curate of
Kirk Braddan (Vicar in 1836). The family thus escaped from
cholera-ridden Douglas, just at the time of a bad epidemic in 1832,
to live at the rural vicarage until Robert Brown's death in 1846.
Kirk Braddan was TEB's home and his school. He placed
"Braddan Vicarage" second in *Old John and .Other Poems,* his
only book of lyric verse. Brown's editors put the poem first in the
collected poems, thus correcting filial absentmindedness.[27] Properly the poem's subject explores the difficulties of a young Manxman growing up and first hearing the accents of England.

TEB's father, Robert Brown, lived all his life on the Isle of Man.
He may have travelled to London to arrange for the publication of
his poems, but no evidence of such a voyage survives. Dorothy

Wordsworth quoted him as speaking of Manx "national honor" and his own poem confirms that this one-quarter Manxman was a Manx nationalist. TEB not only made the journey to England, but he also heard the charm of English accent and lived most of his life in England. Behind his public life in England, however, lived a secret and cherished life of the spirit. His father's voice, like old Anchises', called him to become the "immortal bard" sounding the harp in his native land. TEB became his own Aeneas and his own Virgil to write a comic epic of nineteenth-century Manx life. At the head of his narrative poems, Brown's editors placed "Spes Altera: To the Future Manx Poet," TEB's own thoughts about poetry and his native land. The new Manx poet, according to TEB, would not write in Manx for Old Manx was dying. Although he will write in English, his English will contain "Keltic force, . . . Keltic fire, . . . Keltic tears." The new Manx poet was, of course, TEB himself.

Robert Brown chose TEB's subject: the Isle of Man. His father's poem, with its quaint eighteenth-century diction, proposed also the language problem. Old Manx is dead, but English "Hammered on Saxon stithies," is equally impossible. Even before TEB's birth, Robert Brown began that mingling of souls, soils, and self that produced TEB's Anglo-Manx narratives. TEB, one-eighth Manx, is the Manx Poet.

CHAPTER 2

The Fathers: 1830–1846

> But who shall parcel out
> His intellect by geometric rules,
> Split like a province into round and square?
> Who knows the individual hour in which
> His habits were first sown, even as a seed?
> Who shall point as with a wand and say
> "This portion of the river of my mind
> Came from yon fountain?"
>
> Wordsworth, *The Prelude,* II, 203–10.

WORDSWORTH's declaration that "The Child is father of the Man" particularly applies to Brown because his major writing transformed his experience between his birth in 1830 and his departure for Oxford in 1850. He may have learned much during the six years between 1855 and 1861 when he returned to the Isle of Man, but his Anglo-Manx narratives, all written in England, use characters he knew as a young man and almost all are set in the 1840s. Penetrating the mist of Brown's early life when he knew the characters he recreated for his fiction requires a necromancer like Mannanan McLir. Most information is late and prejudiced not only by personal feeling but also by TEB's professional urge to document "the interesting social phenomena arising from the contact with a civilization [i.e., England] which I hardly call higher."[1] Our first need is to understand the men who served, in effect, as his fathers.

TEB's fiction creates two luminous characters: Tom Baynes and Parson Gale. TEB acknowledged that Baynes contains aspects of himself. Parson Gale is more difficult to trace, but since in every appearance he serves as a father surrogate, a source may be the three men to whom TEB turned for support when he was young.

One father figure is usually enough; Brown had three. His natural father, Robert Brown, was a combative and morose clergyman, Vicar of Kirk Braddan. During the last ten years of his life he was nearly blind, and in August, 1845 (the year before his death), he suffered a nervous breakdown.[2] TEB said he suffered from "the intense melancholy that preyed on the mind and had its source in personal and spiritual experience; it became at last that most terrible of ailments, religious melancholy."[3] Furthermore he spent much of his life in a schoolroom, an occupation taxing on the nerves. With his large family he lived in a small, cramped house on a salary of less than £100 per year.[4] Dorothy Wordsworth indicated how hard he worked. Robert Brown probably never knew his own father, and he was frequently at odds with his ecclesiastical superiors.

TEB's second father was John McCulloch, or MacCullagh, a Scotsman who served as steward for Robert Brown. He lived in a cottage across the road from the vicarage, and TEB declared, "He taught me ... everything."[5] The poem on him, "Old John," titles TEB's collection of lyrics. In the 1830s and 1840s Old John was an old man (born in 1777; Brown's father was born in 1792) with a wife, daughter, and granddaughter. In the poem Brown justifies himself "at Abram's feet" to old John, not to his father:

> To you my life's whole progress would I tell;
> To you would give accompt of what is well,
> What ill performed; how used the trusted talents.[6]

Although TEB does not mention his father in "Braddan Vicarage," Robert Brown appears in "Old John": both TEB and his father need the Scotsman's intercession in heaven!

Brown's third parent was Archdeacon Joseph Christian Moore (1802–1886). When Robert Brown died in November, 1846, only one of his seven living children, Hugh Stowell Brown, was of age. The remaining six children and the widow had to rely on the Manx Church; the agent of this support was Moore. On his holidays, TEB visited Moore, a bachelor, just as frequently as he visited his mother and sisters. Moore was the surrogate parent at that crucial stage when Brown, entering his profession, was seeking a model. Brown called him "a second father."[7]

I   *The Natural Father*

In addition to writing verse, Robert Brown played the organ and composed two hymn tunes. From him, TEB learned to play and respond well to music. Although Robert Brown had no university education, he had the instincts of a scholar.[8] He was an extremely serious man. TEB reported him in deep discussion with Rev. Thomas Howard, his predecessor, and with the Presbyterian chaplain in the next parish, so intent on a conversation that he tried to bridle a cow![9]

He also seemed to have been extremely unstable. In addition to asking Old John to intercede in heaven for himself and Robert Brown, TEB referred to his father's untranquillity:

> Old John, I think you must have met him there,
> My father, somewhere in the fields of rest:
> From doubt enlarged, released from mortal care,
> Earth's troubles heave no more his tranquil breast.[10]

Doubt, care, and trouble marked the man's life and made him, we would say today, psychotic. TEB called him "a born sobber." His crying seemed considerably more than a rhetorical effect to sway a congregation toward virtue and God's true way. It betrayed a fundamental lack of control. TEB said his grandfather in the Guinea trade issued from a severe school of discipline, but he noted immediately that the discipline did not extend to Robert Brown. "Rather it was the profound melancholy of his nature" that marked him.[11]

In a lecture TEB said his father "was one of the most nervous and reserved and bashful of Manxmen."[12] Brown clarified this bashfulness in a letter to his sister. He had found a crayon drawing of his father made by a long-dead brother. A photographer printed the drawing with a photograph of the mother so that they "should look at 'each other.' That would be seemly ... and edifying, however much of an accident in the life of the originals."[13] Robert Brown was also extremely fastidious about cleanliness and style.[14]

Because their father began to lose his eyesight in 1836, first Hugh and later TEB assisted him in preparing his sermons. His sons were "made solemnly and seriously to sit down and read [to him] for two mortal hours."[15] They started on Thomas Scott for theology, turned to David Hume or William Robertson on history, and then to James Hervey's *Meditations among the Tombs* before ending with a poet. The father would sit up late at night meditating, and then "Perhaps at three o'clock the family would hear him playing" on the piano. The sermons in the Manx language were a particular challenge since he had to memorize without genuine understanding. He composed and memorized all his sermons without writing them down, and the Manx sermon had to be tried out on a Manx-speaking parishioner. When he first went to Kirk Braddan, he preached twice a month in Manx, but at the end of his career he was preaching only once in that language. The tension in producing such sermons must have been severe. There was always the fear of a gaffe. "Some words which, if he was not careful in pronouncing, would suggest ludicrous ideas not suitable for the pulpit on Sunday — .... [S]uddenly he would hear a shriek of laughter all over the church."[16] His life was hard and he made it harder; his blindness added further anxiety to the pressures of his occupation.

The Vicarage at Kirk Braddan, although not quite so "close" as the Douglas house, certainly could not be considered spacious. The Vicarage had two rooms on the ground floor with a lean-to kitchen on the back. On the second floor were three small rooms: a bedroom, a study for the vicar, and a room for the three girls. The boys — in 1845 four of them — had the attic room over the kitchen.[17] Brown speculated that the girls may have gone visiting to escape the crowded and tense house.[18] The most graphic description of the life here is from the second son, Hugh Stowell Brown:

[W]hat privations we all, parents and children, had to endure in trying to subsist on the little barren glebe, and the miserable pittance of tithe that fell to the vicar's lot. I will only say that I have seldom seen the children of a Nonconformist minister in a worse plight than that in which I and my brothers and sisters spent those miserable days; when I have seen my mother shed tears of thankfulness and joy, on the arrival of a parcel of cast-off clothing, sent by a Christian lady.... [T]hat parcel, ... coming ... just as the wintry winds began to blow, was hailed with delight.

I have shuddered ... when I have thought of the anxieties that so often brooded over that humble and half-ruined vicarage, where ... a well-educated woman, and a man of learning and refined taste, strove, as working people seldom have to strive, to make both ends meet.[19]

The description recalls Trollope's Parson Crawley in *The Last Chronicle of Barset,* a man nearly maddened by his poverty.

No wonder Robert Brown suffered a nervous breakdown in 1845. His eldest son, a young Robert Brown, was at sea at that time. His second son, Hugh, was in England working as an engineer on the new railroads, and Hugh gave up the job to return to the Isle of Man to help his father. Because Hugh had no public training to qualify him as curate, he entered King William's College at Castletown.[20] In the spring, 1846, however, the Bishop refused to license him as curate for his father, but proposed to send him instead as teacher-curate to Foxdale, a neighboring parish. Hugh was "unamiable and unsympathetic"[21] toward the Isle of Man, but Robert Brown preferred to have Hugh as an unpaid curate rather than to hire a curate using his own emoluments. Instead of following either Bishop or father, Hugh returned to Liverpool to become a Baptist (free from meddling bishops) and to begin a successful career as a Baptist preacher.

In August, 1846, TEB entered King Willliam's.[22] Up until this time, his father had taught him at home. If visits had provided escape for the girls, going to board with his aunt in Castletown may well have been an escape for TEB. Times were uncertain. Manx histories do not mention the potato famine which at the same time ravaged Ireland; the Manx were not so dependent upon the potato. However, such a nearby tragedy might suggest to an impressionable young man the need to acquire an education to suit him for work beyond the Isle of Man. Also, he may have enrolled simply to qualify as his father's curate. His Stowell cousins had done well at clerical careers.

But, swiftly, two cruel blows struck the father. The eldest son, who had followed his grandfather by going to sea, died in the West Indies on October 7, 1846. On November 11, 1846, thirteen-year-old Harry died at home. A contemporary witness reported,

The circumstances of [Robert Brown's] death were peculiarly distressing. He had been very ill, and some attributed his illness to the great sorrow and anxiety he had undergone owing to his son Hugh having left the Church of his baptism and become a dissenting minister.... [At a funeral] Mrs. Weatherall remarked how well Mr. Brown looked considering his recent severe illness. On his return from the funeral, a letter was put into the old clergyman's hands [he was fifty-four]; it contained the news of his eldest son's death abroad at New Providence of yellow fever. A few days elapsed when the Vicar's third [actually his fifth] son died at home, also of a fever. One fortnight after, he himself suddenly dropped dead near his own house.[23]

Hugh's defection to the Baptists may have worried the father somewhat, but he was himself too close to nonconformity to be scandalized. The revival of religious and doctrinal issues would surely have exacerbated his difficulties, however, and may have added an extra strain on his already overstrained life.

The "Memoir" attributes his death to concern for Hugh's well-being. Hugh had returned to the island for the funeral of his brother Harry. He started to Douglas in a snow storm, but the father decided that the weather was too severe for Hugh to risk the crossing to Liverpool and thus started toward Douglas to bring him back. John McCulloch found the Vicar "dead in the snow, not many yards from the Vicarage."[24]

The nervousness, the passion, the strange anxieties point to a man in danger of losing his sanity. His 1845 breakdown, his melancholy pietism, his blindness, and the sudden death of two sons give ample reason for some final tendon to break in November, 1846. Certainly the snow was not the cause of death. Hugh Stowell Brown laconically reported that his father died of a fit of some sort.[25]

The death of a parent is always shattering, but the events surrounding Robert Brown's death must have made it especially hard for his sixteen-year-old son. A family already poverty-striken was thrown on the parish: they had to leave the Vicarage within a month and move in with the mother's maiden sister in Castletown, a woman who had an annual income of £10. There was, of course, no insurance on the father's life; the family was dependent on the Manx Church. If it was a blessing to have the blind old man out of the way, it was an extreme hardship as well, possibly exactly what he had feared.

II *The Guiding Father*

In the confusion, one firm figure, John McCulloch, stands out. The best source of information on him — aside from the poem "Old John" — is a manuscript speech prepared by Joseph E. Douglas for the Brown Fellowship in 1928.[26] Douglas interviewed Old John's granddaughter, a child mentioned in TEB's poem. Old John came to the island in 1795, when he was eighteen, as a farm servant and steward. While he was a steward in Marown Parish (just next to Braddan), he met his wife, Eleanor Kerr. Of his four children, TEB knew only the daughter Robina, who lived with Old John. After his father's death, TEB came back for a visit with Old John and stayed so late at night that the family insisted that he

sleep over with them. In the poem TEB sleeps beside the old Scotsman, just a little bit surprised to find himself there. The poem ends
with this stanza:

> O faithfullest! my debt to you is long;
>   Life's grave complexity around me grows.
> From you it comes if in the busy throng
>   Some friends I have, and have not any foes;
>   And even now, when purple morning glows,
> And I am on the hills, a night-worn watchman,
>   I see you in the centre of the rose,
>   Dear, brave, old Scotchman! [27]

It is a powerful conclusion and a conclusion that TEB never spoke
about his own father. In the poem (dated from Clifton, Dec. 29,
1880)[28] TEB admits the same complexity and weariness that
oppressed his father. Since the sites of Watch-and-Ward to guard
against invaders are still visible on the Isle of Man, the watchman is
no dead metaphor. The thought of Old John as a center of a rose
anticipates Yeats' use of the rose metaphor in the 1890s. Brown
means simply to praise; his words acquire more power because of
later use.

The poem is extremely full of detail. Old John was five foot one;
he came from Galloway in Scotland. He was, surprisingly, not a
Presbyterian — the Doctrine of Election was too severe — but a
Methodist. In the poem Old John relates his epic voyage from Scot-
land, stories of Scots life and literature, and his versions of Scottish
martyrology. He teaches the children rustic lore and manners. Old
John praises Hugh for his ability to pitch hay (the lines are in mock
Miltonics) and brother William's skill in building ricks.
Throughout the poem Old John represents virtue — teacher,
model, hero, and friend.

"Old John" is delightfully comic with absurd rhymes, inflated
and deflated diction, and an antic rhythm that moves like a
scampering dog. The comedy insulates TEB's praise for a man who
is, after all, simply a servant. Laughter also may mask feeling too
deep for tears (or as TEB wrote in a letter, "Too deep for
thought").[29] The comedy proves TEB's strong affection for John
McCulloch. Writing in 1880, master in a good public school in
England, TEB could only express such affection through comedy.

III *The Ghostly Father*

The third parent was Joseph Christian Moore (1802–1886), Vicar of Kirk Andreas and Archdeacon of the Isle of Man (1842–1886).[30] Moore belonged to a family known as the Cronkbourne Moores, from their homestead near Kirk Braddan. Brown wrote to Moore about his hopes in literature.[31] Moore obtained for Brown a Servitorship at Christ Church, Oxford. Moore administered the funds of the family and sent a check and a turkey at Christmas.[32] TEB wrote, after announcing his first position in the class lists at Oxford, that he was pleased to "have in some means fulfilled the expectations" of Moore, a man whose "approbation [he] so highly prize[d]."[33] All the unpublished letters to Moore declare how large the debt to Moore is.

The best picture of Moore's life at Kirk Andreas and of his care for his sons is found in TEB's post-Christmas letter to his sister in 1853, describing Moore, Moore's two collegiate nephews, and a young Manx friend who served as Moore's curate. One nephew was "fresh from Germany — German politics, German literature, German philosophy, German friendships, German wines; nothing but German all over. He amused us excessively by the vehemence of his intonations, and the perfect ferocity of his gestures, ably supported by a mouth whereof thou knowest that it is like unto the crater of Vesuvius. The Archdeacon, who pretended to make fun of poor Jack [the speaker], was really delighted with him, and it was a grand scene when after dinner John came out with some of his political declamations and the old gentleman's mouth (unparalleled as you know save by his nephew's) moved in graceful harmony with the grand convulsions of the ... orator."[34] Like Old John's praying, the Archdeacon's large mouth was available as a subject for affectionate laughter.

In a letter after Moore's death, Brown talked about an earlier Christmas party, in 1848, when Moore and Brown planned the attack on Oxford. In this letter Brown remembered another unfortunate who also came begging, Chalse-y-Killey, the madman.

The Christmas dinner was a scene never to be forgotten. It was held in the large kitchen of the Rectory; all the servants of the household were of course there, besides all those who worked in any capacity on the glebe. The Archdeacon presided. In the midst of all the brightness and happiness a strange weird face was seen at the door, ... Chalse-y-Killey. Chalse was heartily welcomed. There was nothing more remarkable in the Archdeacon than his unfeigned compassion for poor innocents. He seemed to look upon them as children, his own children, and yearn over them with a tenderness curiously blended with playfulness.[35]

Brown noticed the "brightness and happiness" of Moore's house; he never made an equivalent judgment about his own home. Moore had compassion for innocents and treated them as his children, his sons. Moore was "an able and accomplished guide, a grand master-pilot for any waters."[36] His special interest was young men about to take holy orders. In encouraging Brown at Oxford and in giving him an example of loving, intelligent, and gentlemanly behavior, Moore gave the young TEB as much direction, encouragement, and aid as any father.

The contribution of these men was large. Robert Brown's shyness and nervousness as well as his taste and ambition contributed to TEB's character. Blind, impoverished, insecure, emotional, dead under strange circumstances at the age of fifty-four — might the survivors regard his death as blessed release? McCulloch was more of the earth while Archdeacon Moore was the spiritual guide. It is not entirely fanciful to note that this trio was a visible trinity — father, son, and holy ghost. Brown was biological source; McCulloch, the man teaching and acting; Moore, the man of civic and religious duty.

IV *Other Father Figures*

Two other men served as models for the father-figure, Parson Gale, in Brown's fiction. One was William Drury (1808–1887), who succeeded Brown's father at Kirk Braddan. One of TEB's earliest memories was being carried into Kirk Braddan by tall William.[37] Brown reported on events about the Drury family in his letters and called his reports the Druriad.[38] Drury had, like the fictional Parson Gale, two sons. The meaningless entry on Drury in the *Manx Worthies* was written by one of the sons: "The memory of this excellent Manxman will remain in the hearts of his countrymen without assistance from any pen."[39] Vicar of Kirk Braddan for forty years after Robert Brown, he must have been a powerful figure in his community. The few glimpses of him show a man of marvelous common sense. Brown told about a shocked parishioner discovering Drury in a bedroom: Drury said, "Bless me! dear me! if it's a man, what matter, and if it's a woman, ler her skutch somethin' bar her."[40] Drury had sufficient epic spirit to find a place in Brown's Manx epic.

Another prototype for the figure of Parson Gale was William Corrin (1795–1859). Between 1818 and 1825 Corrin was Robert Brown's curate at St. Matthew's in Douglas. In 1825 he went to Kirk Rushen, in the southern part of the island, where he was Vicar until his death. The *Manx Worthies* specifies him as the source of Parson Gale:

A man of many sorrows, for his wife and several of his children preceded him to the grave, he was remarkable for his serene patience . . . shrewd common-sense and his intense sympathy. . . . He entered into the amusements of the young, who spent many happy days "In that old vicarage that shelters under Bradda" [quoting one of TEB's poems], and into the troubles of the old, and he took an interest in the occupations of all, more expecially of the fishermen, who formed a large part of the population of the parish. . . . [H]e was the prototype of 'Pazon Gale' in "Betsy Lee."[41]

As the writer points out, he fits the character of Parson Gale in *Betsy Lee,* but he doesn't fit the character that TEB developed in other narratives. Parson Gale's common sense is chimeric, sometimes surprising more by its appearance than by its regularity.

To these men TEB owed not only a fictional character because Parson Gale seems modelled on them, but he also owed an attitude toward authority. Although Robert Brown seems to have been a difficult man to emulate, TEB fortunately knew men like John McCulloch and Moore. Drury and Corrin, more shadowy figures, also seem admirable and worthy. Is it too much of a conjectural leap to notice that TEB served best as Vice-Principal of King William's College and second Master at Clifton College, but failed when he was Head of the Crypt School in Gloucester? TEB's deference to his headmasters, John Percival (called "Old John") and James Maurice Wilson, was admirable. Both of them strong men, they exacted obedience. Brown seemed uneasy under his final master at Clifton, a more easy-going man. TEB, unlike his brother Hugh, accepted the control of archdeacons and bishops of the Established Church. Tom Baynes, nearly fatherless, deferred always to Parson Gale, the source of aid and comfort not only to Baynes but to his community. Since Parson Gale was equally a figure of fun, again TEB responded with laughter as he did to McCulloch, Moore, and Drury.

CHAPTER 3

Other Voices, Other Places: 1846–1850

I Other Voices

IN the years 1846–1850 TEB crammed his mind with the images for his poetry. The emotions came from his father; the landscape and surface from his years at King William's College and from his mother, his brother, and his sisters. During this period of formal education on the Isle of Man, TEB prepared himself intellectually and emotionally for Oxford. Although he could not have known it when he registered at King William's in August, 1846, TEB was entering the arena he would occupy all his life as a teacher in a public school (in the British sense of that term). King William's College, TEB's school, was a new foundation; the Crypt School and Clifton College where Brown later taught were also new foundations attempting to bring British educational system at one fell swoop from the sixteenth to the nineteenth century. At raw, unformed, and new King William's, TEB began to tolerate a life of outward drudgery to support his inner life of the spirit. He had already learned the need for drudgery in his family.

Robert Brown was nervous, emotional, and unstable, but TEB's mother, Dorothy Thomson Brown was strong, intelligent, and very stable. Although her mother and father were from Scotland, Dorothy Brown was probably born on the Isle of Man. Joseph E. Douglas reported in 1928 that people who knew her called her a "dour person," but the phrase, so often applied to Scots, may indicated fixedness of purpose. Douglas wrote, "I am inclined to think that the stronger and severer nature, the dominant and commanding figure was the mother."[1] She had to be strong, for she was left a widow with six children ranging in age from seven to nineteen years and without an income except gifts from the Manx Church. Selwyn

Simpson, the earliest student of TEB's verse, said that she was "an enthusiastic reader and a great lover of poetry. Besides literary talent [he doesn't specify what talent], she had a great fund of mother wit and humorous originality — of an unusually daring and masculine character — and strong practical commonsense."[2] Simpson, writing early in the twentieth century, may have talked to people who knew her. Brown corroborated her strength of character when he wrote in 1886 on the death of his brother Hugh, who was, he said, "his mother's own child.... [S]he was a great woman. A pure borderer she was — her father a Thomson from the Scotch side, her mother, a Birkett from the Cumbrian side of Cheviot. I don't suppose the earth contains a stronger race, and she had all its strength."[3] A photograph TEB discovered of her in 1893 called to his mind the "intellectual force" which he said was characteristic.[4]

Her force seemed also to involve ambition or an assumption of gentility. When TEB was preparing a speech on Robert Burns, he wrote to his sister thanking her for the mother's judgment on Burns: "I don't remember about the 'vulgarity' but I do remember how she disputed his originality. The vulgarity is the point which is new to me. It is eminently characteristic."[5] She might have looked askance at Burns because of her own class position:

Mamma's view on Burns may have been largely influenced by the Jedburgh "Kritic" of her father.... Our grandfather must have been very little younger than Burns [b. 1759]; and he belongs emphatically to the Scott country. I can well imagine that when Scott rose on the very heel of Burns, there would be a party who questioned the supremacy of Burns.... "Sir Walter was a gentleman" and Sir Walter glorified their own countryside. Just in proportion as our grandfather came under the influence of feudal conditions and the great families (Buceleuch and so forth), and had a touch, however slight, of gentility.[6]

The Manx sometimes wish that TEB were more gentle. In both the Manx and the mother, one senses a desire to be thought better than they were.

Many of TEB's letters to his mother from Oxford were about money. In November, 1850, he wrote to borrow some money for college expenses and concluded "and of course you can pay yourself out of any money that may come into your hands on my account."[7] In another letter, he replied to his mother's suggestion that he apply to the Elland Society for money. Brown refused because in order to qualify he would have to permit an investigation of his religious views. "There's many a poor brick I dare say, who finding his finances at a low ebb, might also discover to his surprise some fine morning that his opinions happened (bless me how nice!) to chime exactly with those of the Elland Society; let such get what they can get."[8] Brown could not afford to be so proud, but surely such a response proves a busy, anxious mother always working to insure the well-being of her children.

The mother had pride and strength and maybe something more that lashed out in TEB's character at critical moments in his life. In one letter to her, TEB spoke of the family tendency to satire as if she shared it; he thought the tendency "the common *curse* (shall I call it) of our family. [We] have a keen sense of the ludicrous and an instinctive dislike of the mean and contemptible."[9] In the same letter he spoke of a "conscious superiority" to the majority of mankind who are "silly selfish boobies." Surely in using such words to his mother, TEB knew he was speaking to a kindred spirit. Strength of character seems certain. Dorothy Thomson Brown was nearly eighty when she died; she was buried at Kirk Braddan beside her husband.

One is on less certain ground in trying to discover what Brown's brothers could have contributed to his definition of self. He mentioned his brothers Hugh and William in the haying scene of "Old John." In his Oxford letters, he referred to his brother William being at sea, and in 1853 or 1854 William settled in Australia. His brother Alfred, nine years younger, was a worry in the Oxford letters, but he too left England for Australia.

Hugh Stowell Brown seemed an absolute antitype to TEB. Not only did he dislike the Isle of Man, but he also had "no poetic ear or vision." Hugh distrusted poetry "as so much gloss upon, or tampering with, fact." Hugh saw the Isle of Man "in the cold, forbidding, desolating light of a November morning, when a clammy mist is coming up out of the sea, leaving him chilled to the very heart."[10] When Hugh spoke of the island, he said, "The genuine Manx people were not remarkable either for temperance, diligence, or cleanliness. They were in these days [his childhood in the 1830s and the early 1840s] chiefly small farmers, whose land was most wretchedly neglected, and whose houses and homesteads were utter horrors of discomfort, disorder, and filth."[11] In his *Autobiography* Hugh said little about his family, leaving the whole subject of genealogy to his brother. Douglas, he wrote, "was full of dirt, and bad smells, and but for the tide which swept the filthy harbour and carried away the offal from the shore, Douglas must have been almost pestilential."[12] When William Wordsworth was in Douglas in 1833, the year after the ten-year old Hugh was moved to Braddan Vicarage, he wrote a sonnet on the cleanliness and purity of the water![13] Hugh deplored the drunkenness. English families, he said, sent their alcoholic younger sons to the Isle of Man, for the liquor was cheaper and thus they "would soon finish themselves."[14] It is not surprising that one of TEB's pleasant tasks in his last five years on the Isle of Man was to take Hugh's children about the island to introduce them to the delights of Manx life.

Hugh was seven years older and clearly his road differed from his brother's all his life. He had started a career as an engineer before he served a Baptist congregation. TEB's letters (now in the Manx Museum) are nearly always mutilated when Hugh's name or Liverpool enters. The first sentence in the following quotation from a letter dated Nov. 13, 1850, is not blotted, except for the name, but the rest is all crossed out. The reading of the rest seems accurate, however:

I wrote to Hugh too upward of a month ago, and no answer yet. I suppose they don't want me at [Myrtle Street?] and therefore keep at a respectful distance. If this be really the case, I shall write once more to Hugh. And if I receive no answer then I'll have great doubt whether I can ever call on him when passing through Liverpool. I should have liked very well to spend the whole vacation in Liverpool, but not as a tolerated bore.[15]

He didn't spend the holiday with his brother; he crossed to the Isle of Man, but on the way back to Oxford, Hugh was violent.[16] Later the tiff was patched over, for TEB did stop regularly in Liverpool on his way back and forth from Oxford. Hugh at the time was establishing himself and the father of a growing family; he may have been just too busy to answer his brother's letters. Other letters report more congenial visits, but nevertheless one feels that Hugh did not need the rest of the family. A late commentator thought the wives were in opposition.[17] When TEB wrote about quarreling sea captains, he called the story "Captain Tom and Captain Hugh."

Irwin said in his memoirs that TEB "always spoke not only of his brother being far better known than himself, but as though he deserved to be."[18] Hugh was widely known as a preacher and an apologist for nonconformist views. *Allibone's Dictionary,* the closest thing to a *Who's Who* in the nineteenth century, gives equal space to Hugh and TEB. In his forty years at the Baptist Church Hugh created a powerful force of social ministry. He instituted Sunday lectures and church magazines for working men. His sermons were published in nine volumes. In 1878 he was elected chairman of the Baptist Union of the United Kingdom.[19]

The differences between the brothers ranged from the proper attitude toward the Isle of Man to questions of church government and policy. They are anti-types — one poetic and romantic and the other prosaic and practical. One had a fine sense of humor; the other none. Apparently a family gene for rhetoric and a family gene for ambition fell on the two men as a gift from the mother. Not surprisingly, the same genes drove the two men apart.

Because Brown's letters to his three sisters were sent home to the Isle of Man, many of them have survived. His sister Dora died in 1855 (she was twenty-eight). His sister Harriet is mentioned in a letter in 1862, but she seemed to have died shortly after her mother. Margaret, four years younger than TEB, survived him; letters written to her, because they frequently discuss family matters, have been most often quoted here. The girls may have suffered more than the sons as a result of their father's early death; they had only gentility to separate them from the ordinary citizens. Margaret married a Congregational clergyman, John Williamson, who seems, from the references to him in TEB's letters, to have been a charming man. Brown never mentioned any children when he wrote to her. He did write asking for her memories of Kirk Braddan and he arranged, especially after his own wife's death, to spend vacations with Margaret.

Margaret shared her brother's interest in the Isle of Man and his ear for gossip. Since she was the last surviving member of the family, she was the source of late information. She told Selwyn Simpson, author of a 1906 dissertation on TEB, that Parson Gale was based partly on Robert Brown and partly on William Corrin, Vicar of Kirk Rushen.[20] She did some writing on her own. In an 1893 letter TEB thanked her for sending him a magazine, probably her husband's parish magazine, which printed her article on "parcel night" at Kirk Braddan. Both Robert Brown and Hugh Stowell Brown referred to this humiliating event at Kirk Braddan when members of the parish brought cast-offs for the Brown family. Unlike Hugh and Margaret, TEB said that the scene was "more humorous" than she stated it.[21] From the hints one gleans from Margaret's letters, she had her mother's strength of character and more stability than either Hugh or TEB.

II *Other Places*

When we turn from the informal education to the formal tuition that TEB received, voices disappear. Brown used the name of his grammar school master in "The Christening," but only his name, not his character. Dr. Dixon, the Principal at King William's, appears dimly in TEB's early letters. Brown's Oxford letters gossip and chatter about fellow King William's College men at Oxford and Cambridge, but only rarely do his associations develop. One school friend, W. Fowler, president of Corpus Christi College (Oxford), officiated at Brown's marriage, but only one letter between them survives.[22] TEB was contemporary at King William's with Frederic William Farrar, afterwards Dean of Canterbury and author of a popular schoolboy novel, *Eric, or Little by Little,*[23] but TEB made little impression on him. The novel's characters are English schoolboys and not one native Manxman appears. TEB's enrollment overlapped James Maurice Wilson's at King William's; Wilson (1836–1931), a remarkable man, served as TEB's headmaster at Clifton. In later life — after a career of incredibly muscular Christianity — Wilson became a one-man agent for TEB's verse. He knew "Betsy Lee" by heart. Although an immense personality himself, Wilson failed to personalize men he remembered; his friends served chiefly to recreate himself. His *Autobiography* is rather forbiddingly devoted to "the Growth of his Religious Thought," but since to him "Life meant action, and there were so many things to be done, such urgent need to do them, that action could not be delayed,"[24] even that subject is considerably fascinating. Wilson and Farrar provide evidence of place and thus, by accident of evidence, this examination shifts from emphasis on characters to the school Brown attended between August, 1846, and March, 1849.

Since Brown's father was the master of the Douglas Grammar School from 1817 until 1834, he was perfectly capable of educating his own children. TEB attended the parish primary school at Port-y-Chee where Edward Creer was master. It would have been expected, since Robert Brown had gone there, that he would send his children to the Castletown School, a school supported by diocesan funds.[25] Bishop Barrow had established the fund in 1668. The original trust had been to use the income from a farm near Castletown to maintain "two scholars at the University of Dublin to be trained for service in the Manx Church, and, after the supply of Clergy for the Island was sufficient, 'then to what other public work or charity as shall by my Trustees be thought to be most profitable to the Island.' " The income had been used to pay masters at the Castletown school, but in 1830, since the value had increased thirtyfold, the trustees decided to apply the fund for purposes of

a College in this Island for General Education, in which the various branches of Literature and Science are to be made the subject of instruction, and the minds of youth imbued with a knowledge of religious truths and moral duties.[26]

A subscription for a building fund was initiated in 1830, and by August of 1833 the building had been completed on land near a Manx landmark, Hango Hill. When King William IV was solicited for subscription, he replied that he could not give money but he would give his name.[27] When the school was opened in 1833, the father of James Maurice Wilson was the first headmaster. The school burned in January, 1844, but by August of that year, it was repaired and back in operation. Forty or fifty boys were then living at the school, which had a total of one hundred and fifteen scholars. That year (at the age of 20) Hugh Stowell Brown was one of the students entering the reopened school.

Robert Brown was opposed to the establishment of King William's College. Frederic William Farrar's *Eric, or Little by Little,* or the *Autobiography* of James Maurice Wilson makes his reasons for opposition clear. The Castletown School served the island; King William's College attracted students from England and Ireland. The rates would be lower than any comparable school in England, and thus impoverished English parents could afford to send their children to the school. The advantage of a cheap English school was also obvious to Irish parents. Robert Brown might well fear the changed mission of the school. In addition to hating bishops, he deeply hated strangers.[28] Although Robert Brown feared the denativizing of the Manx boys, the influx of English and Irish boys was perhaps more beneficial than detrimental since students learn as much from each other as from their masters.

The school from the beginning had a distinct air of rawness about it. Wilson reported that his father was appalled when he first saw the school.[29] In 1838 the walls were still not finished, and they were not finished for a long time; furthermore the walls sometimes leaked two or three gallons of water on a rainy evening.[30] Scholarship was nearly absent. Wilson won a French prize because he alone recognized the French text as the Ten Commandments.[31] Although Wilson and TEB both won the Latin prize at the school, Wilson's English tutor, when he moved on to an English school, smiled grimly at his Latin prose.[32] Wilson also claimed that the school kept his solutions "of ordinary quadratics of two unknowns" in case a future student should reach "such a high-water mark."[33] No wonder TEB had trouble with mathematics at Oxford. The teaching, Wilson continued, "was as bad as it could be."[34] One memorist concluded that TEB's "own force of will" secured his entrance into Oxford rather than the teaching at King William's.[35]

But, bad as it must have been in comparison to English schools, King William's College offered a better education than the old Castletown School had offered. Both Wilson and Farrar compared the school with English schools. Wilson later went to an English school and he became a master at Rugby and headmaster at Clifton. Farrar when he wrote his book was a master at Harrow. Rugby, Harrow, and Clifton were considerably better, but to what would one compare the Castletown School? King William's men of TEB's generation did well at Oxford and Cambridge. When Brown won his Double First, he claimed in a letter to Archdeacon Moore, "the tutors themselves have said that I occupy the same place relatively to the new system that Sir Robert Peel [Statesman and Prime Minister] did to the old."[36] His friend, W. Warde Fowler, also won a first class, and another King William's man, William Howard, won a fellowship at Sydney Sussex College at Cambridge at the same time Brown won his fellowship at Oriel. Despite the bad teaching, something was accomplished.

Wilson, indeed, says that his final two years at the school were his best because then he was left alone to do his own work. King William's might have had the same effect that Hawkshead School had for Wordsworth. Both schools ranked well down in the academic order of schools, but both gave boys a chance to develop their own talent. Both schools had superb natural settings. Both were far enough from academic centers of power so that academic pressures would not reach the point where boys learn only how to pass examinations and rarely how to live. No one, I think, was killed by academic drudgery at King William's College, but a boy was killed when he fell from a rock seeking birds' eggs.[37] For all the dirt and bullying that Wilson complained of, one suspects that he would have been bullied at many other schools and dirt is something that a finicky boy ought to learn to live with.

Brown, even from his first entrance in the fall of 1846, boarded in Castletown and was thus classified as a Day Boy. TEB's contemporaries remember little of him after school hours. Wilson, when asked in 1900 to recall TEB at King William's, said TEB was pointed out "not without awe" on a visit from Oxford. The boys thought TEB knew more than any master and that he wrote "the best Latin prose that the University examiners had ever seen."[38] Wilson's comment on his own Latin, quoted earlier, makes one doubt any high level of achievement. In 1853 or 1854 Wilson said, "The great Oxford scholar [i.e., TEB] spoke to the promising schoolboy, and a life-long friendship began."[39] The friendship is separated from the school.

TEB could hardly have done much work his first term since two of his brothers and his father died that autumn. He left the school in March, 1849. During the summer he continued his reading and worked with Archdeacon Moore to plan the assault on Oxford. That autumn he went to Oxford to sit for the examination by which he gained admission to Christ Church. On the twenty-second of October, a long, full letter to his mother described events during the busy week and a half between Friday, October 12, 1849, when he left Castletown to go to Douglas to catch the ship, until his return to Liverpool.[40] He was so excited on Friday night (he had "a most rascally night at Aunt's") in Douglas that he couldn't sleep, and heavy weather turned the normal six-hour boat trip into nearly a twenty-hour one. He spent Sunday and Monday with Hugh and caught an early train to Oxford on Tuesday. He was

satiated with the beauties of the country and starved to death. I instantaneously made a rush upon St. Edmund's Hall, where after climbing an infinity of stairs, I encountered Joe Kewley [a fellow student at King William's] in the dark sallying forth to meet me. With him I took a jolly strong cup of tea, which considerably revived me, and in a short time we sang "The Messenger Bird" to the great comfort and edification of all and sundry of the tenants of the neighboring apartments.

That night TEB was permitted to sleep in the Hall, and the next day he went to the Deanery of Christ Church to be examined.

The details of the examination would only be tiresome to you; suffice it to say . . . that it took place in the Hall of Christ Church, a most magnificent affair (N. B. the hall, not the examination), and that after sitting from 10½ to 2½ old *Gaisford . . . and surliest old man I ever met with* called me up and told me I had got a servitorship.

The italicized words in the quotation have been blotted out, but a careful reader can make out the letters *ford* in the name and the judgment. Thus TEB met the villain of his Oxford experience. In 1895, he recalled the scene in a causerie on Robert Burton's *Anatomy of Melancholy.* He described Burton at Christ Church and wrote: "How well I remember that library! my meeting there with the great Gaisfordius — a terrible encounter!"[41] It was terrible at the moment, but his later experience at Oxford with Gaisford made it even more terrible and a fit subject to remember for forty-five years.

At the moment, however, Gaisford had instructions:

At the same time he informed me that he was not sure when I would come into residence: possibly not for a 12 month: though, I fancy, this was only to prepare me for the worst; for from his manner of speaking, I should infer that probably I shall be called into residence much sooner.[42]

TEB went into residence in January, 1850. In the letter dated October, 1849, he told his mother how he met his tutor, Reverend Edward Stokes, a Student (i.e., Fellow) of Christ Church, who prepared a course of reading to be followed in the period before he should come into residence.[43] TEB borrowed a gown from Kewley to appear for the matriculation ceremony in order to defer the expense of buying one. He saved money one night in a free bed at St. Edmund's Hall, but the next day he had to find an expensive bed at an inn. He ate no dinner for the entire period that he was away from Liverpool.

His letter has the high good spirits of victory. He told his mother that he would stay in Liverpool a day or two longer in order to celebrate. The education at King William's made possible the successful admission even if most of the effort were his own will. New roads opened before him. His Barrow fund Exhibition (from the trust fund of the seventeenth-century Manx bishop) would pay some of his expenses; the Servitorship would defray living costs. The chance for work in literature that he mentioned to Archdeacon Moore now seemed possible. Indeed, old Oxford had opened her doors once more to a poor boy of parts who would be willing to work and sacrifice for the gift that Oxford gave. If King William's was a makeshift institution and poor aid, no one could deny what Oxford gives her sons. The pretensions to gentility of his mother's family were being vindicated; in one instant he had equalled his brother Hugh. Dorothy Thomson Brown, living with her sister, three daughters, and a still younger son, must have felt some sense of pride as she finished reading the letter, passed it around, and then carefully saved it. A beginning had been made.

CHAPTER 4

Oxford Ivy That Seres: 1850–1855

"Pines are the hardest sort of tree to
live when shifted to any other soil."

Old Manxman in *Moby Dick*

I N October, 1849, Brown's object was "not a degree at any price
to cover my nakedness, but the acquisition of academic learning."[1] With Archdeacon Moore's help, Brown got his opportunity
to fulfill his ambition. The Oxford drama is the first drama that
may be said to belong properly to his own life. His father's death,
the family poverty, his brother Hugh's defection to the Baptist
ministry belong to the family drama. Since Brown greatly desired
the matriculation at Oxford, the wounds — social, religious, and
psychic — that he suffered at Oxford were, as much as they may be
for any man, the result of his own decision. Oxford tried to deraci-
nate him; it nearly succeeded until, just at the right moment, TEB
began to write verse again after a long abstinence from writing.

John Percival, Brown's headmaster at Clifton College, and later
Bishop of Hereford, judged Brown's Oxford life in the acerb and
exact manner that made him a successful school administrator and
ecclesiastic. Percival, an Oxford man himself, knew exactly what
Oxford did to Brown. Percival recalled first meeting Brown in
Oxford at St. Mary's Church, across the road from Oriel College
where Brown was once a fellow. Percival wondered if Brown had

thoughts of his own struggles and triumphs, and of all the great souls that
had passed to and fro over the pavement around him: and all set *in the
lurid background of the undergraduate life to which he had been condemned as a servitor at Christ Church.*

His father's well-intentioned friend the Archdeacon of Man [Moore],
knowing the scanty resources of the Manx parsonage and the need of econ-

omy, but apparently not knowing either the temperament or genius of the
boy, had advised his going as a servitor to Christ Church; and purblind
teachers let him go, instead of sending him to some such place as Balliol,
where he might worthily have been enrolled as one of the most highly
gifted of her scholars.[2]

Percival is being fanciful in imagining what might have been had
TEB gone to Balliol or even to Percival's Queen's College. Brown
thought that being a Servitor was something like being a Sizar, a
very respectable title, at Cambridge. Being a Servitor was, on the
contrary, a humiliation.

The November, 1868, issue of *Macmillan's Magazine* printed
"Christ Church Servitors in 1852: By One of them."[3] It was TEB's
first national publication, but he signed the essay "BETA" rather
than by his own initials TEB. The experience rankled still; he
explained the "dismay, ... indignation, and then smouldering dis-
gust and hatred" that resulted from his being condemned a Servitor. Also in the summer of 1868 Brown had written his earliest surviving manuscripts in the Manx Museum and the earliest dated
poems in his *Collected Poems.* The essay on Oxford and his poetic
production are bound inextricably together.

The essay "Christ Church Servitors in 1852" is one long, sustained cry of pain. Brown's position in the college compares
roughly to the life experienced by American Blacks at many American universities. The position must be the same for the African in
Moscow or the Pakistani in London. The Servitor was an invisible
man, "crushed under the dead weight of an absolute unconscious-
ness of his presence." The Servitor wore a special gown which
could not be disguised. He dined forty-five minutes after the other
undergraduates and Students (at Christ Church the Fellows are
called Students). Brown lived in basement rooms far at the back of
the college. Friends at other colleges would not call on him in fear
of social ostracism; members of the College would not be seen in
his rooms. At divine services, Servitors sat in "a kind of horsebox
railed off" from others. Gentlemen Commoners of Christ Church
ridiculed Servitors as "scribs," and TEB suggested that the epithet
derived from the fact that Servitors could be hired to copy lines
imposed as punishment on the gentlemen. For a crowning blow,
Christ Church refused to admit TEB as a Student (i.e., Fellow)
even though he earned a Double First. When tutors and one of the
canons approached Dean Gaisford in support of the Servitor, the
Dean replied, "A servitor never has been made, and never can be

made, a student." A Servitor lived in the promised land and learned its rules, but he had to keep his peace, wear a mask, and accept repression. When he became a Fellow at Oriel College, Brown was taken to the Union: "I might have been a Cambridge man, or a graduate of Yale College, Massachusetts [TEB's error], being lionized over Oxford." At Oxford and at Christ Church TEB "was a stranger in a strange land."

I   *The Servitor*

It would have been safe for Brown to enroll at Trinity College, Dublin, as many young men training for the Manx clergy did. Or he could have lived with Archdeacon Moore in the bachelor rectory at Andreas while he read in preparation to take orders.

Clearly he had ambition. Selwyn Simpson printed six juvenile poems Brown wrote, two of them dated just before or just after he went to Oxford.[4] His unpublished Oxford letters occasionally mention working on poems. Those poems that Simpson included are conventional in thought and method, but the fact that they are so conventional indicates Brown's pretensions. He was aiming at full cultural statement even if he had only learned, so far, feeble imitation. In his Oxford letters, he prepared himself for examinations and worried not that he would be plucked (failed) but that "people do form such extravagant expectations of a poor fellow: not only people in the Isle of Man, but here too, expectations which I know I can't fulfil."[5] He reported sickness at each examination: he was violently ill before both of the School Examinations and, after he won his Fellowship at Oriel, he was too ill to attend the celebration dinner.[6]

Christ Church was, for several reasons, a surprising choice. Even if he had not been a poor Manxman, the choice would have caused trauma. Christ Church was first founded in 1525 when Cardinal Wolsey set about to construct what he called Cardinal College.[7] When Wolsey fell from power in 1529, he asked King Henry to support his work. King Henry VIII's College was founded in 1532 in the building that Wolsey had put up, and in 1545 the establishment of modern Christ Church was accomplished. Unlike other Oxford colleges, Christ Church is an adjunct to the cathedral. The Students at Christ Church (in contrast to the Fellows at other Oxford colleges) were paid employees of the cathedral chapter (instead of being self-governing Fellows). Christ Church, in the eighteenth and early nineteenth century, was the "aristocratic college *par excellence*." The college history reports that in 1845, "an American Quaker, taken by Mr. Penn [to dine with the Canons of Christ Church], recorded with complacency that all the guests except Mr. Penn and himself were lords." Since the year 1763, thirteen prime ministers of England have been Christ Church men. Between 1797 and 1931, eleven Christ Church men were rulers of India (as the official Guide book has it). John Ruskin was at Christ Church just before Brown; Lewis Carroll was a student and Alice Liddell's (of *Alice in Wonderland*) father was the Dean who succeeded Gaisford. Ruskin wrote, "The greater number of the peers of England, and, as a rule, the best of her squirealty, passed necessarily through Christ Church."[8] Brown was in the wrong place.

The Commoners of Christ Church, England's peers and squires, deigned no glance toward Servitors, but the grievance Brown wrote about in his *Macmillan* essay was already past history. Brown said in a footnote at the end of his essay that Prime Minister William Gladstone, who served on the University Commission which eliminated the category of Servitor, wrote twice to him about ameliorating the condition of Servitors. Brown's stated aim in writing the essay was "to paint ... a picture of a social phenomenon which many ... will hardly imagine could have drifted down so far"[9] into the nineteenth century. The conclusion is lame, but we can imagine a sub-text from the other materials remaining of TEB's life. He suffered because he was associated with trademen's sons. He suffered because the college servants treated him badly. He suffered isolation from other members of his college. Oxford forced him into drudgery and privacy. In a contemporary letter he wrote, "A servitor to be respectable must have some ability, and above all, some considerable industry."[10] Ruskin is more laconic and more brutal: "the servitor's tenure of his college-room and revenue depended on his industry."[11] Brown was learning that drudgery to which he devoted his life so that he could live the private life of the spirit in his poetry.

It is easy to imagine Brown's situation because it is reenacted every time that a young man in a colonial society begins to rise above his fellow students and catches the dream of attending the great institutions of learning which are the open sesame to equality in the modern world. By prodigious efforts of family and friends, he sacrifices what needs to be sacrificed to enter Oxford or Cambridge; or Harvard, Columbia, or Berkeley; or Moscow. At home he was a prize pupil, but at the new institution he is just another bright boy who is, likely as not, actually less well prepared than perfectly ordinary men who make no sacrifice to attend. Brown got only a second class in Moderations, his first college examinations. A critic in 1929 commented, "the unpolished scholarship of his earlier training probably kept him out of the first class."[12] Cut off from social life with other undergraduates and from life with eight of the other Servitors whom, as tradesmen's sons, he would consider of a lower social rank, Brown's only recourse was to sit in his cellar room in Canterbury Quadrangle, at the very back of Christ Church, and study, and hope for the revenge that he sought.

Even Oxford could make some slight admission, however. In May, 1855, when Brown applied to the Trustees of King William's College to secure the position of Vice-Principal at his old school, George Marshall, Student and Censor (the chief executive officer of the Students) of Christ Church, wrote in support of Brown's candidacy:

Under the new Examination Statutes Mr. Brown was the first to gain great distinction in the University, and *under disadvantages which would have dismayed anyone of less energy,* he obtained the highest honours in both branches of the final Examination....[13]

The admission is small, but it is an Oxford admission.

One final point about his social position. In unpublished sections of a letter to his mother from Oxford, TEB mentioned a recent illness:

I really cannot with any face appear in public, in as much as my illness is accompanied with a most goodly company of those unhappy eruptions which are the very pest of my life. As long as I am subject to those things, I shall never know what true comfort is.[14]

He was a Servitor living in the cellar. He was Manx. He had pimples!!

II *TEB and the Oxford Movement*

Since Brown was sent to Oxford through the offices of the Manx Church, he owed service to the church in return. In accepting the money from the Barrow Fund, Brown entered into an agreement that he would carry out the aim of the Trust to provide clergymen for the Manx Church. He did not enter the Manx Church. Was his failure to serve a lack of opportunity or a rejection by the Manx Church?

In letters written in 1853, during his last year at Christ Church, Brown was clearly looking forward to returning to the Isle of Man to become a curate. He expected ordination up until November of 1853, just before he finished his final schools examination. In the spring of 1853 he wrote a long, painful academic letter to a clergyman on the Isle of Man, seeking to remove any taint of the Oxford Movement.

Brown's commitment to the Manx Church did not waiver. Thus he wrote to secure an "eligible situation" on the Isle of Man; "as I have no definite prospects anywhere else, I should on the whole be happy to accept such an appointment."[15] In November, 1852, he had written to his mother about his obligation to the Manx Church:

I have been thinking a good deal lately about my connection with the Manx Church, and put the matter as I will, I can not see how I can honestly fulfil the obligation under which I lie with regard to it without actually doing all that I can to procure a situation in that church. I really do not think that even the paying back of the money is any adequate compensation. The church in the Isle of Man calculates, and has a right to calculate on our services. We are in fact (there's no disguising it) *her* servants, to be disposed of as she thinks proper. I am resolved. . . .[16]

At that point the letter breaks off. Clearly he wished and expected to return. He had no other possible means of paying back what the church had advanced.

He accepted money from the Barrow Fund. At the end of 1852 he reaffirmed his obligations. Even earlier, in April, 1851, during his second year at Oxford, he refused to apply for money from the Elland Society because he feared it would compromise his position as a member of "the Church of England, and matriculated at the University of Oxford."[17]

On the fourth of April, 1853, he wrote to his sister Margaret: "Now I am likely to be ordained to some place on the Isle of Man about Xmas next, and shall probably have a house and shall want a housekeeper."[18] From the same letter it is clear that he was engaged to marry Amelia Stowell. On November 30, 1853, when he was still waiting to take his second examination, he wrote about leaving Oxford within two weeks. "I don't think though that I shall be in time for an ordination on the 18th. And I fancy they can put it off a week surely."[19]

Not one of these plans was realized. Ordination was simple, comparatively speaking. TEB had only to present himself to a bishop for examination and the proper ceremony. However, he could not become a priest (i.e., priested) until he had an assignment to a parish. Brown was ordained at Oxford (and not on the Isle of Man); he was not priested until 1884, some thirty years later. What happened?

At Oxford Brown became involved with religious views that hindered or totally blighted his chances for preferment in the Manx Church. The High Church Party (or Tractarians, or Puseyites) began at Oxford in the early 1830s under the direction and influence of John Henry Newman, Hurrell Froude, and other Oxford men who wished to emphasize the continuity of the English Church and its sacramental character. In their view, the English Church had only separated politically from Rome. They sought to revive the sacraments of the church, including a greater use of incense, music, and the ancient offices. These men spread their influence by means of "Tracts for the Times." Ninety of the Tracts were published in the 1840s with phenomenal sales. The last pamphlet, written by Newman, argued for the continuity of the English Church, and declared the protestantism of the English Church was a mere vagueness of language to sustain the Elizabethan settlement between the radical Puritans and the conservative English churchmen. The uproar was so great that Newman stopped the publication of further "Tracts" (his bishop ordered cessation). The movement was considerably reduced in its effectiveness by the publication of Froude's *Remains,* which made clear that Froude had gone toward Rome, and finally by Newman's reluctant decision in 1843 to leave the English Church and to be received in 1844 as a Roman Catholic. While splintered, the movement had power at Oxford during Brown's undergraduate years, for Oxford continued to discover the beauty and meaning in the sacraments. Repeating the ancient offices and reviving ancient traditions gave the young men at Oxford a greater sense of contact with God than working to collect money to print Bibles or to establish Sunday schools. Fitting and proper music at a service seemed as important as visiting the sick. A beautiful service was more fixed and certain than a sermon which might or might not be edifying.

The question of Brown's churchmanship may seem much ado

about a minor nineteenth-century tizzy, but in fact the English-language literary tradition is almost entirely a High Church tradition. TEB's father's verse was Evangelical, and pious, and terribly dull. Of Low Church writers, one thinks only of John Bunyan, Daniel Defoe, and possibly John Milton. Milton carried from his childhood a High Church tradition of form and design. Bunyan's energy sustained an art form that is as simple as a sermon. Defoe wrote tracts in fictional form. The High Church tradition, with its sense of form, design, and ritual, frees the artist to experiment with life in works of art. The Evangelical is too serious, too close to experience, and too anxious. The Evangelical does good work; art may distract him. Most Evangelical writing resembles, if anything, the grim productions of Social Realism in the Soviet Union. Only the High Church tradition seems capable of playing with experience to produce proportion, shape, and beauty. Brown's transformation at Oxford not only made him unfit for the occupation as priest in the Manx Church, but it prepared him to write his Manx narratives. Oxford made him an exile, but Oxford enabled him to comprehend and shape the memories he carried with him into exile.

The historical situation of the Manx Church complicated TEB's situation. The Manx bishop is not subject to the Archbishop of Canterbury. Because of visits and support from the Wesley family in the eighteenth century and because of Manx national pride, the Manx Church in Brown's time and in the twentieth century is more Low than High Church. Joseph Christian Moore, Archdeacon of Man, TEB's advisor, was himself strongly Low Church as was Robert Brown.[20] Brown said that Moore was "absolutely free" of the Oxford Movement.[21] Manx churchmen, as well as many churchmen in England, were very suspicious of the Oxford Movement, but the Manx had an additional motive in their suspicion of all things English.

To be sure, in his letters to Moore, Brown reported that he "detested" the Tractarian party,[22] but Brown would make every effort to separate himself in Moore's Evangelical eyes from the Oxford Movement. Also in a letter to his mother in 1851 Brown fronted the question of High Churchism directly and, in effect, admitted its attraction. Brown had been ill but his two friends, Prosser and W. Warde Fowler, came to his room to have tea with him and to report what had been happening in university life during the two days of Brown's illness:

Prosser is perfectly infatuated with High-Churchism: it is absolutely
ridiculous, but then he's just the sort of creature to go with streams. There
is a majority of Tractarians at Oxford. Therefore Mr. Prosser must be a
Tractarian. . . . This morning he was describing with enthusiastic approval
a church in which he had been on Sunday, and in which amongst other
munuments, he had seen a large stone cross erected over the "altar," with
a crown of thorns around it! ! ! Fowler's High Churchism is of quite a different stamp; it is grave, serious, and conscientious. . . . Fowler's views,
like my own, have undergone some modification, since last term: the
danger arising from the machinations of the Jesuits — which both he and I
at one time regarded as a mere bugbear appears now both to him and to
me a startling reality. They actually boast of the number of men whom
they have in Oxford as Tutors! ![23]

Surely the letter admits TEB's attraction to the Oxford Movement,
or Tractarians. He must have known that the cross with the crown
would produce a *frisson* in the good, Manx heart. When he
defended Fowler, Brown probably defended himself. No event in
the spring or summer of 1851 might have made Brown and Fowler
more aware of the machinations of the Jesuits. The idea of Jesuits
among the tutors at Oxford is too Elizabethan to be serious, but
since only seven years before Oxford was shaken to its foundations
when Newman became a Roman Catholic, Brown's explanation
might have been satisfactory to an Evangelical mother on the Isle
of Man.

Selwyn Simpson argued, on no particular evidence, that Brown
developed religious doubts at Oxford which paralyzed his action
until his poetry could resolve those doubts.[24] *Doubts* is a word to
cover much territory; the letters show no doubt except for interest
in the Tractarians. Simpson did not see the letters quoted here, and
his study pays little attention to the religious ferment at Oxford. If
anything Simpson is Evangelical himself, making an Evangelical
analysis of Brown's poetry. James M. Wilson's sour and grudging
introduction to Simpson's "Appreciation" acknowledges that,
while admirable in intention, Simpson misses the point.

In 1930 one of Brown's friends on the Isle of Man, the novelist
and churchman, John Quine, made an astonishingly clear analysis
of Brown's problem, and his understanding supported the contention that the Oxford Movement caused Brown's difficulty and prevented him from being a Manx clergyman. Quine also suggested
that Brown's position was his position throughout his life as he

remained suspended between the two demands of the church.
Quine said that there were

two opposite, or rather incompatible, conceptions of the Christian ... at
this time [at Oxford] brought into prominence in heated controversy. In
effect [Brown] had to decide as to his choice; or otherwise decide if he
would concern himself with neither. From earliest times the Catholic
Church ... imposed two distinct concurrent functions on its priesthood —
to minister forgiveness of sins to sinning humanity; second, to minister
consolation to humanity in its sufferings, privations and sorrows. But in
the Church of England, the former of these functions of the priestly office
had long been in abeyance. The Oxford Movement begun in Oriel College,
demanded that the Church, through its ministers should again minister
forgiveness to the sin-laden as well as comfort to the sorrow-laden; and for
both these ends teach mankind the mystery of sacramental grace.

This idea of sacramental grace would hardly be spoken in Manx
churches. In Man, mystery is talk about faeries. The church has
more serious business. Quine continued by placing Brown precisely
between these two demands:

Mr. Brown stood between the claim of one party and the repudiation of
that claim by the other. Not through timidity or any inferiority complex,
nor through pretensions to be superior to these agitations; but through an
understanding of himself he stood observant. He knew that to exercise the
ministry of the forgiveness of sins some men are absolutely unfitted;
though all the same, well endowed to exercise the ministry of consolation
and sympathy. For whatever he thought of the former need, there is end-
less need of the latter ministry to this vast mass of humanity that is fated
and pre-destined to privation and suffering. He understood the apostolic
saying: there are diversities of gifts. But at the same time, he was pro-
foundly aware of the part played by "make believe" in religion; and especially of that widely prevalent notion about "forgiveness of sins," wherein
people are persuaded that they may minister absolution each man to himself and claim to be forgiven. He was acquainted with the desiccating
blight of this notion; and to it he extended no sympathy and could concede
it no connivance. ... That interior revolt was the index finger pointing to
his own social destiny.[25]

Quine knew Brown only during the last five years of his life on the
Isle of Man, but his discussion is further evidence that Oxford ren-
dered Brown unfit to serve the Manx Church. Oxford taught him
the idea of sacramental grace, which the Manx Church could
hardly conceive. At Oxford, he found himself between two worlds.

In February, 1853, Brown wrote to a Manx curate to allay suspicions about his High Churchism. The letter is as important as the *Macmillan's* essay, and it admits that his High Church Tractarianism is the thorn in the flesh:

Should the Archdeacon [Moore] or Mr. Christian [Vicar of Sulby] be at all apprehensive on the score of my (supposed) High Churchism, you are quite at liberty to show either of them this letter, as a kind of exponent of my views, as far as a poor enquirer like me can be supposed to have any views.[26]

From the beginning Brown sought to be agreeable, to be what the Manx Church wanted him to be. He had been warned, evidently, that Sulby was a hotbed of Methodism. Brown, therefore, preferred "a set of people who will fearlessly, perchance bitterly, avow their objections to the Church system." He was confident that he could meet a Methodist challenge on intellectual and emotional grounds. On the prejudiced man he believed he could

force upon that man the conviction that the very indifference which he affects to *forms* and ceremonies, for instance, is the very reason why he should be a churchman: for I could show him how that these may be seen, underlying all forms, that pure and vigorous current of Christian life which in every age and church and country has been and is, steadily setting for the eternal interests of man.

In the very teeth of opposition to sacraments, Brown argued for them and proved their need. He would try to sink into the community, he wrote, to know why Dissenters were so powerful there. He would try to see things as they really were in the parish and try to adapt his course of action "to the particular emergency." He climaxed his protestations about the need to understand the Church in its actual relationship in the following highly rhetorical voice:

O that men would see this more clearly! that they would consider that the Church was made for man, not man for the church; that *men* were not made to be squared and disciplined by unvarying inflexible ecclesiastical forms, but that the forms have been instituted as instruments which men might use for the everlasting good of their fellow creatures.

I am afraid you'll accuse me of writing an essay, not a letter.

He was, of course, writing an essay.

And the essay was artfully done. His arguments were the arguments of the Tractarians, the High Church Party in the Established Church. His arguments, however, also flattered and praised the Manx Church, if the reader wants to read them that way. His argument said, in effect, "you can't defeat the Methodist by becoming a Methodist yourself." The forms of the Church must grow out of the community in which the church exists, but they must be forms. He was, in short, trying to have his cake and eat it too.

The letter was equally astonishing in its close. Brown vowed his eagerness and willingness to work with Mr. Christian.

His views on many points I have observed coincide exactly with my own, especially one which I have heard him unfold very lucidly: I mean, the propriety of the Church's acting as a kind of corrective in politics: e.g., treatment of the poor, the fatal error of supposing that the Church is to stand aloof from the political world, an error which amounts to a denial of the validity of an establishment.

Brown was speaking at the very nub of contention between the Evangelical and the Sacramental party. The Evangelicals had a long tradition of social service; in their eyes, the sacramentalists were turning away from mankind's pain and privation. Brown's argument was extremely sophisticated, and it was carefully planned to mollify Manx fears. He supported the forms and ceremonies of a Manx Church, but his reasons were toned-down arguments that Newman and Pusey and other ritualists in the Anglican Church affirmed. The letter proves his "(supposed) High Churchism" at the same time it attempts to placate the jittery, provincial, Evangelical fears.

Brown, sent to Oxford to prepare himself to serve the Manx Church, found himself incapable of serving that Church. He was not ordained by the Manx Church; Sulby found a curate elsewhere.

If anyone had doubts, it was Robert John Eden, Bishop of Sodor and Man. In TEB's long letter to Moore in December, 1853, telling about his Double First and his rebuff for a fellowship at Christ Church, Brown said that he preferred a pastoral career, but he acknowledged the possibilities of a career at Oxford. He ended the letter by asking that Moore join him when he confronted his Manx Bishop: "I should also like to call upon the Bishop, and have a personal explanation. If you would kindly accompany me I should esteem it a great favor."[27] He must have been asking for an explanation of why he would not be ordained and priested.

His next letters were depressed. In January 1854, he wrote disconsolately to his sister: "I've no doubt you've heard from Mamma that I'm what they call an Oxford Double First. I'm now looking about to see how this may be turned to advantage. As yet it has not done much for me."[28] There is no further mention of her being his housekeeper, no mention of his engagement to Amelia Stowell. He did not explain. He simply did not become what every step in his life had led toward. If the victory at Oxford was a bitter moment in Brown's life, the failure to return to the Isle of Man may have been equally bitter.

Two years later Wilberforce, Bishop of Oxford, ordained Brown. The Wilberforce family was at the beginning of the century a great power in the Evangelical branch of the English church, but as the century wore on the family became more High Church.[29] During Brown's tenure at Oxford two brothers and the brother-in-law of the same Bishop of Oxford went over to Rome. During his last two months at Oxford, Brown filled the pulpit for one of these Wilberforces.[30] Brown probably needed the money to cover moving expenses back to the Isle of Man; he came home ordained in the English church.

III *Poetic Beginnings*

Brown wrote in the *Macmillan's Magazine* essay that men without society, will manage somehow,

but as long as they live will feel the consequences in a want of social strength, in a tendency to suspicion, to isolation, in an exaggerated self-reliance, which with them is scarcely more than self-denial, in a love of solitude which, unless the heart-springs are very full, must come to little better than moping.[31]

This striking sentence states habits that marked Brown's life after Oxford. He lacked social strength and ease; he was uncertain how far to presume or how far to assert himself. His suspicions cost him a career at the Crypt School in Gloucester. His isolation at Clifton College was so complete that few of the masters reported directly about him in their memoirs; instead of joining in the masters' society, Brown was more apt to take long walks on Clifton Downs, the wide expanse of country adjacent to the school. His exaggerated sense of self-reliance set Brown to writing long dialect poems which were, in effect, self-denial. If he wrote in English, he must be judged by the standards of English verse; if he denied himself English verse, he wrote, in effect, in solitude. The final word in the *Macmillan's* quotation, *moping,* seems at first almost ludicrously inappropriate. Brown's typical method, however, was to rise to a climax and then dissipate the climax. In both his life and his poems, TEB would rise to a moment of climax and then retreat. The vigorous autobiographical energy of the *Macmillan's* essay (TEB's *apologia pro vita sua,* as in Newman's title of his autobiography, but without Newman's religious development) prefigures the direction of the poems that Brown was just beginning to write. Oxford isolated even further a man already an alien (and a victim of pimples).

Brown might not have won a Double First if he had been ordinary. Alone in his basement rooms in Canterbury Quad, he simply drudged. He continued to work after he received his Double First to qualify for election to an Oriel Fellowship. Oriel College was distinguished for its scholarship and intellectual culture. Within a year Brown applied for the position of Vice-Principal of King William's College. One memoirist quotes friends as saying that TEB "never took kindly to the life of an Oxford Fellow" and that TEB had no desire to "fatten on a Fellowship."[32] John Percival says that Brown yielded "to the impulse of his romantic Manx temperament, ... married his cousin and turned his back on Oxford."[33] Oxford and Oriel were useful to him; the Oriel Fellowship gave him entrance into the world, but neither blemish nor distinction of scholarship marked Brown. For all his Oxford Double First, he taught on the Modern Side at Clifton, teaching English literature rather than Latin. Like any good Victorian, he employed tags of Latin and Greek. In "The Parson's Story," TEB retold the Demeter-Persephone myth with a perfectly straight face as if it were indigenous to the Isle of Man. TEB was neither antiquarian nor scholar. He read Dante and Ariosto, but he showed no sign of the compelling curiosity that might mark a scholar in classical literature or in law. One paragraph of A. E. Housman on a problem of classical scholarship compared to Brown on Dante shows a Brown not interested in language or history but interested in the human question.

The historian of Clifton College writes, "Few of us knew that he was a poet."[34] His poetry was part of his inner cherished life of the spirit and not a matter for public display. The boys at Clifton, when they did hear Brown's poems, thought them "quaint and amusing."[35] As the *Macmillan's* essay says, "God only knows what your young Englishman can do under the influence of a tradition."[36] TEB did not write in their tradition and thus he would be amusing and quaint. So Brown at Oxford learned the game of outward conformity in order to succeed at examinations and at his teaching career.

Oxford may have given him one other disappointment. Selwyn Simpson prints poems written before Brown went to Oxford. TEB mentioned literary ambitions in his letters to Archdeacon Moore. In unpublished Oxford letters he mentioned writing a particular poem. In April of 1851, he wrote that he had given up "trying for the poem; it was too late, and besides I left at home the scrap which I had composed before leaving."[37] He seemed to be working for a deadline. He mentioned the same subject again in the fall:

I go quietly working on, steadily keeping the end in view. The poem, however, is in progress, and with the help of such inspiration as I may catch on the old shores of our Isle during the vacation I hope to bring it up here next term complete. As far as it goes I rather feel satisfied; but when it is finished I shall submit it to the opinion of competent judges, Stoke[s] among the rest, though there are some undergraduates here whose opinion in such matters I should prefer to that of the whole Hebdomadal Board.[38]

The published text does not print the next paragraph which again mentions a poem.

Yesterday I set up the first picture of any kind that I have introduced into my rooms. It is a portrait of that fine fellow Kossuth, the Hungarian patriot of whose arrival in England you should be glad to hear. It is said that he will come up to our commemoration; if so he will hear the prize poem recited, whoever recites it, and if possible some tribute of respect and admiration should be at least hinted at. The portrait is a lithograph, and a present from a friend of mine here. I think I shall have it framed or glazed.[39]

It sounds very much as if Brown unsuccessfully competed for the Newdigate Prize for poetry at Oxford, but there is no record of submissions for the contest. John Ruskin and Matthew Arnold won it. The monetary reward was small, but the greater reward would have been the honor. Brown did not mention a long poem again. The only poems of his that survive from his Oxford days are the translations, "Callimachi Hymnus" and a chorus from Sophocles' *Ajax,* along with an original funereal poem, "Chorus of Angels" (dated October, 1850), on the arrival of a child in heaven, and a conventional statement on "The Love of Christ." None fits the category of a prize poem. The translation from *Ajax* is partly in octosyllabic couplets, and prize poems were required to be in couplets. The meter is the same later used frequently in the Manx poems. The prospects for literature at Oxford did not quite materialize. Was he too shy to offer his work?

It is just possible that TEB wrote the following verse published in the *Cliftonian* for July, 1884. It is signed with the name Brown, but it could be the work of a student in Brown's house or even another Brown at the school. Still, the words and wit seem characteristic of him, and, in view of his statement to his mother about a competition, possibly his:

> A poem in English hexameters, complaining
> about same

> Yet indeed did I strain for success in the Prize Competition,
> Manufacturing rhythm in terrible metrical wonders,
> Which, when after I read, I shrank from inflicting
>   the horrors —
> Horrors were they, in truth — on the ears of
>   the luckless Awarder.[40]

Thus TEB may not even have submitted his entry for the Newdigate Prize.

"Manufacturing rhythm in terrible metrical wonders" was not far from TEB's actual practice. His Manx poems are written in an eight-syllable rhymed couplet; although the couplet is difficult to write, he manages both rhyme and rhythm to great comic and narrative effect. TEB's English poems tend each to have a different metrical scheme, but they are all rigidly structured. Surprisingly, nineteenth-century British writers did not free themselves (as Whitman did) from rigid poetic design even though they had a theory, dating from Wordsworth, about poetry reflecting the speech of real men. Arnold's "Dover Beach" is free verse, but Tennyson's *In Memoriam* is in a tight four-line stanza rhyming *a b b a.* One suspects this metrical control links with the control that the Oxford Movement found in perfect recitation of the Eucharist. The insistence on religious forms parallels the frenetic insistence on poetic form in Tennyson, Swinburne, and, at the end of the century, Thomas Hardy. Once a reader is free of twentieth-century prejudices about freely evolving speech rhythm, he or she can appreciate that within their rigid metrical wonders, nineteenth-century poets could achieve significant results. The measured speech of TEB's Manx rustics may please more than his more free, but sprawling, English poem, "Aber Stations"; in the English poem, the freedom has simply dissipated the poem's energies. Brown needed "metrical wonders" as much as he needed the forms of the Book of Common Prayer.

When TEB did publish at Oxford, he published anonymously. The British Museum Library and the Bodleian at Oxford both hold an anonymous pamphlet, *The Student's Guide to the School of 'Litterae Fictitiae,' Commonly called Novel-Literature,* printed at Oxford and published in Oxford and London in 1855. The pamphlet is a mock outline for a course of novel reading with sample exam questions on Trollope and Dickens. It is ascribed to Brown and another Oriel Fellow, Henry Earle Tweed. The publication was discovered by an accidental "lighting upon a paragraph in the Manx Sun of 20th Jan, 1855."[41] The journalist notes that the *Evening Mail* of January 5th praised the work, "a joint production of our young distinguished townsman, Mr. T. E. Brown."[42] The work was also reviewed in *The Times* of January 4, 1855, and a second edition appeared before the end of May, 1855.[43] The pamphlet is an amusing *jeu,* a game, on the century's major art form and on Oxford's serious forms of examination. Typically Brown used humor to comment on "your young Englishman . . . under the influence of a tradition." In an unpublished letter to his sister Margaret, TEB asked that she look up his friend Tweed at Lincoln Cathedral.[44] He said nothing about their joint literary efforts, but at least we know that they were friends.

The outward dates of the Oxford experience are plain and simple enough. Brown went into residence in January, 1850. In the autumn of 1853 he completed his examinations and looked forward to ordination and priesting in the Manx Church. He was neither ordained nor priested probably because of suspicions of his High Churchism. In April, 1854, he was elected Fellow at Oriel, but on May 12, 1855, George Marshall wrote from Oxford to King William's College to recommend Brown as Vice-Principal. On May 15, 1855, Edward Stokes, Brown's "good, kind, genial" tutor who was "radiant with his own happy innocence, sweet, loving, and beloved" (in the *Macmillan's* essay), wrote in support; on May 16, 1855, Edward Hawkins, Provost of Oriel, recommended Brown as a "modest, amiable, well-principled man, extremely well-adapted to the duties he would undertake in your college."[45] Thoroughly changed and altered by Oxford, TEB came back, if only for a moment, to his own soil.

CHAPTER 5

Schools: 1855–1897

I'm here at Clifton, grinding at the mill...
O ... broken life! O wretched bits of beings,
Unrhythmic, patched, the even and the odd.
    "Clifton," *Poems,* I, 72.

THIS chapter completes the story of Brown's outward "kapelis-tic" life as a schoolmaster. From 1854 until 1892 he lived with pupils, first because it was a profession in which he hoped to advance and then because it was an occupation to sustain his inner being. As a Fellow at Oxford in 1854 he had pupils, but in autumn, 1855, he became Vice-Principal at King William's College. In 1861, he became master of the St. Mary le Crypt School at Gloucester, but in August, 1863, he precipitously resigned to become master of the Modern Side at Clifton College. Speaking to a Clifton friend and fellow master, Brown defined three periods in his life: "The Isle of Man mastership, the Gloucester episode, and the Clifton dream."[1] How dreamlike Clifton actually was depended upon the audience to whom he was speaking since Brown was often disenchanted with Clifton drudgery, "longing" to be in fact or in spirit on the Isle of Man. Pupils get on the nerves of masters, and all three of Brown's life segments are marked by signs of nerves which the inner life might heal.

Writing late in life, Brown advised a young friend not to waste time; he had wasted twenty years of his life "to mere idling" instead of writing.[2] The one period that fits his judgment of idling is that between the autumn of 1849, when he matriculated at Oxford and the summer of 1868 when he began to write again. He was hardly idle outwardly, however, because in this period he strenuously devoted himself to his profession as a schoolmaster. This is the one period in his life when the outward life fully occupied his attention. Because the outer life failed, he turned to the inner life of genuine activity in 1868.

I   *The Isle of Man Mastership*

In a letter to his sister on June 10, 1855, Brown announced his plan to leave Oriel College and return to his homeland:

I am going to leave you see, and am booked for Castletown, there to abide until further notice. I feel quite jolly about it, and have no doubt of its turning out well. Don't listen to people who talk about my throwing myself away and all that nonsense. They know nothing about it.[3]

Clearly someone had talked about his throwing himself away. Three motives seem possible: (1) Money continued to worry him; (2) he had fallen in love with Amelia Stowell and become engaged to her while still an undergraduate, but a Fellow of Oriel could not marry; (3) and he needed to fulfill his obligation to the Manx Church.

One of Brown's friends, A. W. Moore, wrote about the return to the Isle of Man,

His Oxford friends urged him to remain at the University, declaring his "attainments were altogether beyond the requirements of the Isle of Man," but he, feeling very properly, that his exhibition from King William's College laid an obligation upon him to offer himself for the service of the Church in the island, felt bound to do so.[4]

Not one of his Oxford letters of recommendation — from Stokes, Marshall, or Provost Hawkins — made such a judgment. But if Brown could not be priested, quite obviously he could serve as a schoolmaster.

While Brown talked about ordination and a curacy, he did not tell his mother about the appointment at King William's until after it had been made.

With regard to the Vice-Principalship (for such it is, not second mastership), I hope you are not [angry] at my silence hitherto. The fact was that I thought it just possible I might not be the successful candidate; and therefore I wanted you to have it in your power to say that you didn't know whether I was a candidate or not.[5]

Now that a decision had been made and announced, he defended his action:

I don't know what you may think. But I am in great spirits about it. I have no doubt whatever about the step; and observe it is only part of a more extended plan. My Brother Fellows congratulate me. Their only draw-back being the fact of my withdrawing to such an out of the way place. But as a preferment (temporary, initiative, of course) they all consider it most eligible.[6]

He is not as strong in this as in the letter quoted earlier written on the same day to his sister. The "extended plan" might refer to the Manx Church, but it might also refer to Amelia Stowell or to some plan of using educational occupation, as Thomas Arnold had used it, as a stepping-stone to another career. Brown promised no extended service; the position, as he later said, started him back toward England. He was going to the quiet limit of the world to make, once again, preparation for another attack. His letter to his mother continued:

There were fifty-six candidates, many of them distinguished men, several Fellows of Colleges. This may serve to show that as things go, £200 a year, even in the Isle of Man is not a thing to be sneezed at. In fact, the educational market is fearfully overstocked, and there is no demand proportionate to the supply. The consequence is that really good men are eager to catch at anything. The term Vice-Principal is happily selected. You've no idea what an impression it makes here. Now just cast your eyes onward a few years, and estimate the effect of this [illegible] upon my future application for higher preferment in England.[7]

He was defending a move that his mother might doubt or else he would not be at such pains to explain and justify it. He ended the letter by telling her that he would spend a fortnight of his coming vacation in Ramsey, a week in Andreas, and the remaining time at Castletown preparing for his new responsibilities. Miss Amelia Stowell lived in Ramsey; Archdeacon Moore lived at the Rectory, Kirk Andreas.

Brown might have returned to serve the Manx Church, to provide more ready money for his mother and his sisters, or to marry. What other opportunity might be open to him? He was ordained at Oxford.[8] He reported taking a pulpit during the summer while

Oxford friends were on vacation, but he had no charge. What could a young man of promise do?

A. W. Moore and Quiller-Couch report that William Gladstone offered Brown political work but that he refused.[9] No letter of support for this offer exists. On January 6, 1878, Brown said to his friend, J. R. Mozley, "Politics move me not. There is nothing architectonic in this science."[10] Gladstone was the member for Oxford after 1847. He became Chancellor of the Exchequer in December, 1852, a position he held until February 22, 1855. Gladstone was a Christ Church undergraduate (he is given credit for the 1867 reform in Brown's *Macmillan's* essay), and he might well have been kind to a Double First from his own college. However, no one mentioned what the offer might have been or when it might have been made.

Whatever the cause, about August 1, 1855, TEB entered on his duties as Vice-Principal of King William's College. Few letters survive since most of those to whom he often wrote lived nearby. There is one report of his life at Castletown; Flaxney Stowell (a distant relative) organized an evening school in Castletown for which Brown was headmaster. Stowell wrote:

He was a genial man. . . . In the evenings he would come to our Temperance meetings, and sit quietly in a corner of the room. When he got home he was not so quiet, for he would mount a chair and imitate every speaker he had heard at the meeting, mimicking all their humour and peculiarities, and reciting their speeches word for word. Doubtless these meetings would have something to do with the development of his humour in after life, when he rose to eminence. Many a familiar turn of speech and thought in his writings was gleaned in this way in his early days spent at Castletown.[11]

James Maurice Wilson spent an Oxford vacation with TEB at Derbyhaven and they boated and walked. When Brown spoke at Castletown in 1895 about his memories, he said nothing about the College but the walks, boat expeditions, and the night school figured in the talk. The College Register for the years when Brown was Vice-Principal shows very few boys leaving for Oxford or Cambridge. Dr. Dixon, who had been the headmaster when Brown, Farrar, and Wilson were students, continued in the post. Dixon seems not to have inspired Brown in the slightest. In an 1893 lecture Brown said that he feared Dixon when he was a student,[12] but his comment on Dixon looks like a determined effort to speak well about a man who had little to recommend him:

Now Dr. Dixon had to manage the Squireens who came to King William's because of the low fees, and many people did not see how admirably he did it, but the fact is that in carrying out his methods, he was prevented from becoming in the Isle of Man what nature had meant him for — a very great favourite, a man of delightful good humour, a man of tenderness indescribable. He had to be severe.[13]

Dixon sounds like a man who showed no tenderness, who had no humor, and who was not a favorite. At another time, TEB said he lacked "sweetness and gentleness."[14] Dixon was not the man to transform King William's College.

An 1858 novel, *Eric, or Little by Little,* by Frederic W. Farrar, a former student at King William's, has also been blamed for the stalemate in college growth. Published one year after *Tom Brown's Schooldays,* Farrar's novel went through thirty-six editions before Farrar's death in 1903 (when he was Dean of Canterbury Cathedral).[15] The "Memoir" prefixed to Brown's *Poems* accuses Farrar of "fouling his nest" when he wrote the book.[16] In his preface to the second edition, Farrar insists that "no place of education can be identified with Roslyn," his fictional school, and he praises King William's "in terms of cordial eulogy and sincere recommendation."[17] A twentieth-century reader is hard put to understand how the book could (1) have hurt the school or (2) been so popular. It is a seemingly innocent tale of schoolboy games, tricks, and modest drinking. But, at the end of the novel, Eric is dead in retribution for some unnamed sin.

In an early chapter Eric feigns sleep in his dormitory while some other activity, undescribed, is going on, but, the narrator tells us, Eric discovers a new kind of "iniquity" and a poison flows "deep into his veins. Before that evening was over, Eric Williams was 'a god, knowing good from evil.' "[18] What Eric saw and did, Farrar leaves to the reader's imagination. Later when Eric asks his chums why they have not been warned of such danger, one boy reminds him that the headmaster preached a sermon on "Kibroth-Hattaavah" (Hebrew for "graves of the lustful"). English boys have perished and lie buried at Kibroth-Hattaavah; "May every schoolboy who reads this page be warned by the waving of their wasted hands, from that burning marle of passion, where they found nothing but shame and ruin, polluted affections, and an early grave."[19] Patently Farrar was writing about schoolboy sexuality. Brown's friend James Maurice Wilson hints darkly — he quotes a hymn — that sexuality was a problem in the school,[20] but then it was a problem at many schools. Farrar himself was a master at Harrow when he wrote the novel, and he wrote the novel just when the headmaster of Harrow was being cashiered out of the school for his sexual activities with his students. At Harrow no one talked. Farrar knew what sexuality in schools caused.[21] Nineteenth-century readers could translate Farrar's hints and suggestions, and Farrar did place his school on the Isle of Man. Even if King William's College did provide less expensive education than English schools, parents might hesitate to send a son to a school where a boy, as a character in the novel says, was likely to be "spoilt and ruined."

Nevertheless, whatever the disappointments of his work at King William's, during his six years as Vice-Principal TEB soaked up more of his beloved Manx landscape and he did marry. On June 24, 1857, Thomas Warde Fowler, his High Church friend at Oxford, married TEB and Amelia Stowell at Kirk Maughold, the parish church for Ramsey, Miss Stowell was his second cousin and belonged to a numerous and influential Manx family on the northern tip of the island. In August, 1858, their first child, Amy Dora, was buried in the cemetery, aged three months.

II   *The Gloucester Episode*

The Crypt School in Gloucester, in the west of England, was founded in the fifteenth century. A deed of January 11, 1539/40 establishes that the school had been built, but by the eighteenth century the school simply ran down. The fund was still there and the schoolhouse, but the cathedral had its own Cathedral School which effectively outclassed the Crypt School. In 1857, the school was closed, the fund was allowed to accumulate, and by a process established in British law, the foundation was reorganized with new rules and a new board. During the interim, 1857–1861, public hearings were held. From the very beginning of the reorganization, litigious elements in Gloucester threatened the school's rebirth. Gloucester enjoyed educational debate; as late as the twentieth century a master claimed there was a "rooted hatred of everything educational" in the city.[22] Brown's involvement in the discussion in 1861 was disastrous to his hopes of "higher preferment in England."

The period during which the Crypt School was closed — 1857 to 1861 — marked the height of the movement in England to follow the steps of Thomas Arnold, who as headmaster of Rugby had demonstrated that humane and sympathetic teaching could help bring English education in one leap from the sixteenth century to the nineteenth century. Gloucester needed a second school. The Cathedral School had acquired an aristocratic tone; the eternally rising middle class needed the Crypt School for its children. Newspapers report events on the reorganization as if the process were of national significance as indeed it was.

Brown's name appeared as one of fifteen candidates for the post of headmaster on a list of January 3, 1861. By January 15, the list was reduced to eight names and all were asked to come on January 29 for interviews. One withdrew but the other seven were interviewed, and Brown received twelve of the sixteen votes the board cast.[23]

Brown was at Gloucester for the meeting on April 4, 1861, when C. Naylor was selected from six candidates to be Second Master.[24] Since Naylor (he served the school until 1890) came from King William's, he must have been Brown's candidate. Brown had not only to hire his own Second Master, but to engage other candidates for teaching. During the first year, classes were held in the ancient school building while the new building was under construction. Administering this construction was Brown's responsibility in addition to his teaching. He asked the Board to increase its allotment of funds in order to construct a Fives' Court, a playground, and more rooms. By October, 1861, sixty-five boys had been admitted. In September, 1861, the Board paid for an advertisement which listed as "Head Master Rev. T.E. Brown, M.A. Late Fellow of Oriel College" and continued, "Boys prepared for the Universities, the Middle Class, Military, Naval and Civil Service. Examinations and commercial pursuits. Terms £1.10.o / Quarter." That cost for education is just slightly below what one would have paid to buy a three-volume novel. Gloucester, one would think, might have been satisfied with a great educational bargain.

Reading the Minute Book one senses the excitement of new creation. The Board of Governors is asked to consider new applicants for masters and to accept new students. The building and grounds occupy their care and attention.

In August, 1861, the following letter appeared in a Gloucester newspaper:

To the Editor of the Gloucestershire Chronicle Mr. Editor. — I had "taken flattering unction" that when the Crypt Grammar School was opened the systematic book-trade of schools in general would be totally abolished at least in this city. Sorry I am to find that I made a miscalculation. It appears to me, sir, that no two masters can teach from the same text book; no wonder, then, that the boy says, "I cannot read out of another boy's book." Eton will not do at Shrewsbury; Westminster don't suit Rugby; Merchant Tailors' will not go down at Charterhouse; and of course the Crypt and the [Cathedral] College must divide on the same subject; what does for one cannot, by any chance, do for the other. Assuredly it would be a great boon if the Council of Education were to fix the text for all books for all the services even up to the church itself. Parents would then be able to form some slight calculation of the ultimate education of their families. If masters are not sufficiently remunerated for their services let the salaries be raised; but do not *force* men of education and superior talents to eke out a living by joining in the book-trade, making thereby the school *bill* equal to the school *fees*. Locally I beg to refer parents to the "terms" of the new Crypt Grammar School, and caution them to hold it in tact: "All printed books must be found by the parents."

The Crypt is again in its infancy, and this caution, well looked to may save parents who are blessed with large families of sons, an amazing amount of money in the end. I should be glad to see the same books which my eldest son uses, do for my second, and so on until the sixth; but I fear unless a bold stand is made, and the "terms" strictly abided by, such will not prove the case.

Aug. 6, 1861.   Paterfamilias[26]

The nub of the question — which so furiously angered Brown — was the suggestion of Paterfamilias that the masters were making money by the sale of books. The "terms" he refers to are the rules of governance for the new school; the agreement was that parents would buy books directly from booksellers rather than from the masters. Without such prohibition a master who selected from a particular publisher could receive a cutback, rebate, or discount on the cost of each book sold.

Brown was stung to fury by the letter. Another letter writer claimed that Brown soon discovered who had written the letter and, further, had questioned the man's son about it and about his father's motives. Brown dipped his pen in acid and replied:

Sir — As you admitted into your columns of last week a letter reflecting upon me, I presume you will grant to me the same publicity which you have accorded to the individual signing himself "Paterfamilias." Although my assailant has a manifest preference for fiction, I shall state facts; and, denying myself the privilege of following your correspondent into what appears to be, to him, the congenial realm of falsehood, I shall limit myself to truth.

1. It is gross impertinence, and grosser absurdity, to demand of a schoolmaster that he should compromise himself to the books used in any other school, however excellent; much less to the accumulated rubbish of all the garrets and old bookstalls in Gloucester.

2. I am introducing into the Crypt School the books which I have been accustomed to use at King William's College, Isle of Man.

3. These books concide [*sic*] in so remarkable a degree with those in use at the Cathedral School, that the boys who have joined us from that institution have had to get scarcely any new books. Indeed, considering that this agreement is purely accidental, I cannot but consider it as most singular.

4. Nothing could give me greater pleasure than to make my boys a present of the discount upon books. In fact, such was originally my intention; but, as it has been strongly represented to me that such a course would be unfair and injurious to the book trade of Gloucester, I have thought it right to modify my plan in this respect. In some shape or other, however, I hope to make this trifling sum available for the interests of the school generally rather than for my own. Of course, this is my *ipse dixit;* and, of course, "Paterfamilias" will not believe a word of it; and, of course, I leave the public to judge how far a man who has been convicted of one lie is likely to boggle at another. Whether it be native meanness of disposition, or whether it be also long familiarity with kindred baseness which has led your unfortunate correspondent to rush recklessly into this mare's nest, I know not. The obscure workings of such intellects are altogether beyond the scope of my analysis.

It is, at least, satisfactory to the public to know, as they do know now by a flagrant example, how far they are henceforth to place confidence in the accusation of dyspeptic scribblers such as the *gentleman* whose feeble nastiness defiled your last week's columns. To me also it is eminently satisfactory to be able from this time forth to dispense with the disagreeable duty of chastising *anonymous* rascality. *Ex uno disce omnes.* Once for all "Paterfamilias" has his reply, and I hope he likes it.

In conclusion, I gladly turn from so offensive an exhibition of impotent wickedness to all that is manly and generous in this noble old city. To the citizens of Gloucester I say — Here I am: at least let me have a trial; at least give me fair play to start with. I have come among you with my hands pure from any such stain as has been imputed to me. Jobbing and corruption are things which I have not known as yet; and I do not think I shall learn them in Gloucester. With the utmost confidence I commend my cause to all honest men: they will know how to stigmatize the low and cowardly attack which has been made upon me through the medium of your journal. And while I appeal to them I appeal also to you, sir, as the editor of an influential local paper, to exercise a little wholesome discretion in the choice of your correspondents, and to protect me from the insinuations of blackguardism, and the slanders of the slums.

Barton Street, Gloucester, August 15, 1861.

To the good citizens of Gloucester, the debate was almost as good as a novel. The editor reported that all copies of the *Chronicle* that printed the letters were snatched up (even the copies of the competing *Mercury* which reprinted the letters).

What could have been in Brown's mind? Whatever merit he had in his argument, he dissipated it in the quality of his language. Indeed, a master does have the right to select texts. Indeed, he did use many of the same texts that the other school used. We can take his word that he intended to dispose of the premium to the school in some way (he should not have been so vague about the use of the money). Further, the editor of the *Chronicle* pointed out that "Paterfamilias" should have raised the issue exactly one year before when the Court of Chancery approved the Charity Trustees' scheme for the government of the Crypt School. The government plan did take care of just the questions that "Paterfamilias" claimed that it had not disposed of. Brown had a winning case which he effectively destroyed by his vituperative rejoinder. The *Chronicle* editor himself thought Brown's letter not in agreement "with established notions of gentility, or conventional good breeding." The editor thought Brown had forgotten he was the minister of the Established Church.

"Paterfamilias" continued the discussion under his real name of Ambrose Dawson Cookson, a surgeon in Gloucester. He now claimed two aims in his original letter: (1) to "expose the crying evil of the amazing increase of school text books" and (2) to call the trustees' attention to violations of the published "prospectus and . . . rules" in order that the trustees will do their duty. He commented on Brown's language and praised the master of the Cathedral School. He also listed the textbooks required by the two schools and noticed where the Crypt School differed.

The *Chronicle* printed three more letters on the subject, all signed with assumed names and all fiercely critical of Brown. The first, signed "Materfamilias," used vigorous Swiftian invective in which Brown was supposedly praised for his fine Christian charity. Another letter writer said that Brown's letter was a production "which few persons with the ordinary education and habits of self-control, which are supposed to characterise gentlemen, would attribute upon its chance perusal to one of their own class." Another writer said that surely Brown would have learned better manners at Oxford. The editor closed the series by giving his reasons for not publishing another letter in his hands because he now believed that

Brown himself was "conscious of the serious mistake he committed in writing" his letter. The editor said that public opinion was loud, distinct, and unanimous in its judgment of Brown's culpability in writing his letter. The logical course, according to the editor, was for the "Charity Trustees to take official cognizance of the affair." The threat was hardly veiled: Brown should leave.

What explanation can be given? The school term had just opened and the beginning of term was always nerve-wracking. Brown's eldest surviving daughter was born on the 23rd of August; he may have been concerned more than usual. The Minute Book makes clear that Brown's duties were onerous, far beyond the ordinary call on a headmaster. The entire community was watching to see if he could resurrect a dead school which the community needed. The Brown family had a reputation for cantankerousness; his father "hated" bishops and strangers. Brown admitted in an Oxford letter to a family propensity to satire. He knew at Oxford that "it is impossible to keep in with people ... without a little harmless hypocrisy." Mankind, he wrote to his mother, are "silly selfish boobies," but he warned himself that it is "better not to tell them that they are so."[27] Brown forgot his Oxford lesson in Gloucester; he told the boobies that they were boobies. Further evidence of the sharpness of his temper comes in a letter to his mother from Gloucester in 1862:

A very good instance of the sort of bother I am subject to here in my exalted position as Headmaster of a place like this, was brought under my notice this morning. The other day I called a nasty, lazy, ill-mannered young whelp at school "a little hog." Today I received a letter from the father demanding an explanation! ! ! Can absurdity go further? However, I am becoming gradually very thick-skinned. Twelve months ago this foolery would have annoyed me. At present I can laugh at it.[28]

His judgment, even in a private letter, seems indiscrete, but it gives us some clue as to why Brown left Gloucester.

According to the Minute Book, the Board did not take up the question of Brown's dismissal, but discussion must have occurred. According to Brown's letters, he tried to find a place for one of his masters, Francis Cotton Marshall. Marshall was appointed on February 11, 1862, but during the fall Brown mentioned some difficulty in his position. On Feb. 23, 1863, Marshall asked to leave the Crypt School on the following day to assume headmastership of the Bridgewater Grammar School. The trustees were "astonished that

Marshall has been out hunting a new job and set a date for appointment without telling them he contemplated any arrangement."
Marshall ignored their letter and so the board decided that in the
future all resignations would require three months' notice. On
March 30, 1863, William Tutin of Queen's College, Oxford, was
appointed assistant master, but on August 16th he resigned. The
trustees made not the slightest demur. Brown's own letter of resignation was dated August 19, 1863; he asked to be relieved of his
duties by October. It may be of some significance that the trustees'
meeting on August 19th received Brown's annual report but
"resolved to postpone the consideration thereof until a future
date." At the next meeting, August 24th, they accepted his
resignation.

Brown stayed at the Crypt School until October 15. No one en-
forced the three-month period of notice for resignation. In the
spring of 1864, the trustees received a request from the second and
third master who asked for compensation for serving as headmaster during the period after October 15th.

So ended the Gloucester episode. The chief effect was that
Brown had as his student the poet W. E. Henley, who was one of
the boys admitted during the first term the school was re-opened.
Later Henley wrote, "Invictus," one of the best known lyrics in the
English language, which begins,

> Out of the night that covers me,
>   Black as the Pit from pole to pole,
> I thank whatever gods may be
>   For my unconquerable soul.

Henley wrote an enthusiastic essay on Brown after Brown's death,
and he offered Brown the pages of his *Scots Observer* and (under
its later title) *National Observer* where Brown published during his
period of retirement. Henley is the *only* ex-student with knowledge
of Brown in a class room to write praising him as a teacher.

When Brown told his mother about leaving Oxford for King William's, he said that he hoped the move would lead to eventual preferment in England. If he hoped for preferment in English schools,
the future must have looked dark to him as a result of the Gloucester episode.

III   *The Clifton Dream*

The "Clifton dream" began because John Percival, the new headmaster at the newly founded Clifton College, asked a friend to recommend someone for his Modern Side. Percival (1834–1918) had just the career that Brown might have dreamed of. After graduating from Oxford, he spent two years at Rugby and then came to Clifton where he was head from 1862 until 1879. In 1862, he started with sixty boys; in 1879 there were 680 boys.[29] Percival too won a Double First at Oxford and he was a Fellow at Queen's. The Council of Clifton College was promised, before his appointment, that "he would do for Clifton what [Thomas] Arnold did for Rugby."[30] The school historian says that in 1872, when the school was only ten years old, Oxford's distinguished scholar Benjamin Jowett pronounced it "already one of the great Public Schools."[31] He left the school with problems, but he left the school well established. Before he died he had become Bishop of Hereford. Brown might well have had just such a dream for himself when he wrote to his mother on June 10, 1855, that he acted in accord with "a more extended plan."

At Rugby, Percival had known James Maurice Wilson; he asked Wilson to recommend a master for the Modern Side. Clifton, unlike other schools, was to give equal value to its Modern Side. Wilson reported:

I named Brown; and he came over [to Rugby] to be interviewed. He spent an evening at my lodgings. About half a dozen of us dined there. I warned Brown that he must be on his good behavior. He did not take my advice. Never was Brown so great. I still remember the Manx songs with their odd discordant pianoforte accompaniment and final shriek; the paradoxes; the torrent of fun and talk; and the stories: —

Stories, stories, nothing but stories,

Spinnin' away to the height of your glories.

Percival, I think, was the first to leave, his usual gravity having been completely shattered. Next morning I asked him, not without anxiety, what he thought of Brown. "Oh, he'll do," said Percival. And so he came to Clifton.[32]

For all of his administrative talent, Percival had little sense of humor. When he told the story of his first meeting with Brown, about the only similarity between his account and Wilson's is that Percival also admitted that Wilson instigated the meeting. All else is entirely changed:

Mr. Wilson having told me about him, I made an appointment to see him in Oxford, and there, as chance would have it, I met him standing at the corner of St. Mary's Entry, in a somewhat Johnsonian attitude, four-square, his hands deep in his pockets to keep himself still, and looking decidedly *volcanic*.

We very soon came to terms, and I left him there under promise to come to Clifton as my colleague at the beginning of the following Term.[33]

Sidney Irwin, who printed both versions, called this a second interview. The meeting and the settlement had been completed by August 19, 1863, since Brown said in his letter of resignation at Gloucester that he had accepted a mastership at Clifton College.

Percival was the kind of man Brown needed. He was a Cumbrian — Brown and other masters spent summer vacations climbing with him in the Lake District. Brown said that he had a touch of mysticism about him. Another friend said that he would have made a "splendid managing-director of Harrods,"[34] London's largest department store; another that he had the judgment of a "sound man of business with the enthusiasm of an Apostle."[35] His main effort was to preach the necessity of "a corporate life."[36] He was an intense worker, who could "not brook opposition."[37] Brown himself said, "At the end of the term we sink back on our seats and mop our foreheads and pant. He is divine; but we want rest."[38] And like Thomas Arnold, Percival had "an almost morbid sense of the sinfulness of boyish human nature."[39] At Rugby he made the boys wear long shorts with elastic bands in them which held them below their knees like knickers or baseball pants. According to a Rugby colleague, "Percival really did consider that bare knees were indecent and might be an incentive to vice."[40] His manner was that of a prophet; he had habits of marmoreal silence.

When he preached this remoteness gave the impression of melancholy, of a man who bore the burden of a mission, always warring against the sinfulness of boys and the class-selfishness of men, their indifference, their "individualism." So then he would seem to withdraw into himself. He begged the boys to think of the School Library as a place "where the average notions of men, the perishing or misleading voices of fashion or custom, should lose their hold over you."[41]

For just a moment, Robert Brown comes to mind, but the bust of Percival shown in J. R. Mozley's *Clifton Memories*[42] makes him look much more Hellenic than the Hebraic Brown. His best friends sometimes addressed Percival as "Old John."[43]

A somewhat different picture of Clifton appears in Phyllis Grosskurth's *The Woeful Victorian: A Biography of John Addington Symonds.* [44] Symonds' father was one of the founding board members of Clifton College in 1860. He sent his son, John, to Harrow where he knew the blandishments of the headmaster, Charles John Vaughan. Young Symonds participated in Vaughan's downfall; his showing a friend's letters to his father precipitated the scandal. John Addington Symonds spent much time at Clifton. Frequently Symonds and H. G. Dakyns, one of Brown's closest friends among the masters, found themselves rivals for the affection of students at the college. Each summer they would vie to see who would take a boy to the French Riviera or to the Swiss Alps. Frequently a boy described as a great hero in the school history is also a great hero in the lives of Symonds and Dakyns. Brown never once showed any hint of being aware of the sexual play that Grosskurth describes. One of their favorites was Norman Moor, who later became a master at Clifton; Brown wrote at Moor's death:

I can't write, I can think only in one direction. It is terrible . . . I will write soon again. Under these strokes let us creep a little closer together, a little closer together. All this draws my love back again [to Clifton]. I do feel for it, for you, as well as for [H. G. Dakyns]. But the rest is silence. [45]

Symonds gave a series of lectures at Clifton to be near one of his boys, Cecil Boyle, who lived in Brown's house (and was president in 1871–72). [46] Brown never discussed the Hellenic interests of his friends.

Life at Clifton differed immeasurably from life at King William's or the Crypt School. Brown had found a man whom he could follow, and he found congenial friends and activity. The Modern Side, of which he was head, did not develop as it was intended to develop. Percival left in 1879 because of dissatisfaction with the Modern Side, [47] the very work that Brown was set to do. The bright young men were in Classics; after James Maurice Wilson became headmaster, the science teaching improved and also attracted a share of the best students. Brown had the students who remained after the classics and the science teachers had siphoned off the best.

Not only was Brown a master, but he lived in Brown's House, a dormitory for some fifty students of the college. Here his contact with students was a little wider than in his classes. The picture of his life with his wife and six children is never distinct. Quiller-Couch reported arriving at Clifton and being assigned a room at Brown's House without Brown's knowing. He was sent to the drawing-room to await Brown's return from classes:

I heard the front door open, an explanatory voice (female) in the hall, and then, as a French stage-direction might put it, *détonation à la cantonade* — "What! What is it you're saying? ... Murder! Who sent him? I'll have none of it!" (More gentle explanation.) "Oh, very well... But I won't have this fellow from Heaven knows where contaminating the morals of my boys! Since you've admitted him, my dear, you'll just have to put up with him as one of the family!"[48]

Because Quiller-Couch had picked up a book on climbing, Brown invited him to join him the next morning for a walk on the downs.

Brown's life at Clifton seems to have turned on the drudgery of teaching, the drudgery and responsibility of running a boarding house, occasional sermons or lectures on literary topics to the whole school, and short escapes to the Lake District, the Isle of Man, or Switzerland. He had to get away. In 1881 he wrote to a Manx admirer that he was quite surprised to discover him continuing his work at the same steady pace.[49] His holiday letters have the high glee of a man who lives intensely and well for a short period of his life. He certainly held no sinecure at Clifton which would enable him to devote time to the arts. His income was sufficient; one observer estimated it as over £1000 a year, counting both his income from the college and the profit from his boarding operation.[50] He worked for every farthing of it.

Clifton expected work. Percival's muscular Christianity sent him in search of further work. The college sponsored a mission church for working men in one of the poorer parts of the city. Boys contributed to the mission fund and worked at the mission; the masters contributed money and effort also. At this mission church Brown was finally priested as curate in 1885.[51] He never mentioned his duty in the parish in letters; he made no announcement. The school magazine, *The Cliftonian,* reported that Brown sang in the masters' quartet, gave talks at chapel, and sponsored the magazine.[52] He seems in the contemporary records just another master. He went about his business as the others did; part of their business was to be slightly astonishing to the boys.

At Clifton Brown performed with success under the command of John Percival and James Maurice Wilson, both of them captains of their own souls. He was less happy under the headmaster appointed after them. In October, 1891, he wrote to Wilson:

> The term is not a quiet one for me. We have had a horrible affair in my house, quite unparalleled, I think. New forms of iniquity! One can't keep pace with them.
> Glazebrook [the new headmaster] is very nice, much happier. I can't say that I am. These things bowl me over terribly.[53]

One imagines many kinds of iniquities after reading *Eric* or the Symonds biography, but Brown, at sixty-one, was too tired to laugh at them or ignore them as he might have earlier. Under Glazebrook the school seemed to wander. In the spring of 1892 TEB had a long period of illness and so he suddenly retired. He had earned sufficient money (there was no pension at Clifton until 1918) to buy a house at Ramsey, at the northern end of the Isle of Man.

At Clifton four of his children were born (Dora and Birkett were born at Gloucester). His wife died at Clifton in 1888. She was buried in the churchyard of Redland Chapel, a lovely eighteenth-century chapel near Clifton College. In October, 1897, Brown returned to Clifton to visit friends. He was speaking to boys in one of the Houses when he suddenly fainted with a heart attack. He died a day later and was buried too in the cemetery at Redland. Grass grows over the marker. How strange that he should die in his old haunts at his old job and not on the Isle of Man where his imagination always went.

In 1869 he wrote a poem about his drudgery at Clifton; he revised it only slightly to make the numbers right when he published the poem in 1893:

> I'm here at Clifton, grinding at the mill
>   My feet for thrice nine barren years have trod;
> But there are rocks and waves at Scarlett still,
>   And gorse runs riot in Glenn Chass — thank God!
>
> Alert, I seek exactitude of rule,
>   I step, and square my shoulders with the squad;
> But there are blaeberries on old Barrule,
>   And Langness has its heather still — thank God!
>   . . .
> Pragmatic fibs surround my soul, and bate it
>   With measured phrase, that asks the assenting nod;

> I rise, and say the bitter thing, and hate it —
>   But Wordsworth's castle's still at Peel — thank God!
>
> O broken life! O wretched bits of being,
>   Unrhythmic, patched, the even and the odd!
> But Bradda still has lichens worth the seeing,
>   And thunder in her caves — thank God! thank God![54]

The place names are all Manx; the drudgery all Clifton. The poem is a bitter reflection upon his broken life, whether in 1869 when it was written or in 1893 when it was published. The poem poses its opposites so absolutely. In 1869, Brown accepted the duality of his life and went through the paces of being a character and a master at Clifton. In the mornings before breakfast, he told Quiller-Couch, he went for long walks on the downs nearby and composed verses. Few students knew about these poems; the college histories are somewhat surprised that TEB was a poet. The authors, one feels, are slightly put out, but they are proud of his connection with the college. It is also clear that they've read little beyond Brown's title pages. "O broken life! O wretched bits of being."

The poems were written, however, while he ground away at his life as master. The poems sustained his spirit. On an English down, ironically, the Manx national poet walked and thought of gorse, heather, ruins, and lichens; he also invented a comic epic of modern Manx life. In comedy he could treat those subjects "too deep for thought." His real life was in his poems.

CHAPTER 6

Feeling, Doubt, and Fallen Women:
The English Lyrics

The wildered brain,
The joy, the pain —
The phantom shapes that haunted,
The half-born thoughts that daunted.

"Chalse A Killey," *Poems,* I, 12

I N the nineteenth century, critics praised quickening emotion in
their poets and denigrated the measured order and objectivity of
the eighteenth century. Matthew Arnold, for example, coolly dis-
patched most of Pope's verse to the category of prose. The best
nineteenth-century writing — Wordsworth's *Prelude,* the lyrics of
Coleridge, Shelley, and Keats, Tennyson's *In Memoriam,*
Browning's *Ring and the Book,* and novels of Dickens, Eliot, and
Hardy — followed the progress of a soul toward a more open, feeling response to the world. God was dead; in 1859, Darwin insured
that Nature, deified as a substitute, died also. Nearly every writer
was plagued by the loss of old verities but reassured because the
heart could still feel. Tennyson stoutly affirmed in the periods of
the worst grief of *In Memoriam,*

'Tis better to have loved and lost
Than never to have loved at all.

(xxvii, lines 524–35)

In a world with no verities, one certainty was feeling itself. "I feel
and cry; therefore I am," they seem to say. Brown was with his
brother poets in anguish. A poem entitled "Pain" (n.d.) begins:

85

> The man that hath great griefs I pity not;
>   "'Tis something to be great
>   In any wise, and hint the larger state,
>   Though but in shadow of a shade."[1]

TEB wrote of pain in many of his English poems, bewildered poems about phantom shapes and half-born thoughts. They struggle for resolution, closure, completion, unity.

Two features of these poems will surprise readers: first, they employ startling sexual and bodily images. In one poem he imagines that sunsets are the excrement of heaven. Second, Brown sees dualities, from the "joy and pain" of the lines quoted in the epigraph to this chapter to many others: male and female, clean and dirty, Greece and Israel, dream and reality, Clifton and the Isle of Man, sanity and madness, nature and art, England and Italy, Manx dialect and standard English. These oppositions are sharp and, as in the poem "Clifton" (1869), absolute: here and there, me and them. The poems used the word *God* to articulate some resolution of all these opposites. As "great griefs" will "hint the larger state" (see "Pain" above) so out of suffering these oppositions may resolve into a unity. The nineteenth century tried many definitions of God (Arnold's "not ourselves tending toward righteousness," leaps into mind) and TEB too attempted to define the Unity. Sometimes he named God; in successful poems he realized God.

I   *Feeling in a Dry Land: "that our souls live"*

Brown published his English lyrics in *Old John and Other Poems* (1893), but at least one fifth of the poems in that collection date from 1868–69. Between 1870 and 1875 he stopped writing English poems. In 1875, he wrote English poems to be published in the parish magazine of his brother's Liverpool Baptist Chapel; these poems may have triggered a second creative period between 1875 and 1881 or 1882. Brown's readers can not see this development because the poems are printed in absolute hodgepodge order in *Poems* and they are not dated.[2] This discussion of TEB's lyric poems follows the chronological order of their composition to see how Brown starts in absolute dualities and slowly moves to some kind of reconciliation in the idea of human perception, human understanding.

We start with a conventional poem with a conventional opposition. "The Pitcher" (July 1868) contrasts a container standing in a flowing stream to a speaker who is himself dry and empty. "God's sweet fountain" no longer pours generously over him as the stream pours over the pitcher. The questions are, of course, why has the water stopped and will its flow be renewed? In the last two stanzas, a completely extraneous "God of goodness" is introduced to answer the questions. The closure, the completion, the resolution comes from outside the poem. The speaker concludes that his soul deserves its dryness because it is both torpid and small:

> "Not so!" saith the God of goodness;
>   "I have many souls to fill;
> From this soul a while desisting,
>   I will tarry in the hill.
>
> "Then, when it is dry and dusty,
>   I will seek the thirsty plain;
> I will wet the mossy channel,
>   And the purple slate again."   (II, 327)

The wasteland, one wryly notes, is not usually so easily slaked. The theology — that the soul receives grace without merit — is unexceptional. The poetry is weak. Brown does not specify "the walls, altar and hour," as Gerard Manley Hopkins does in the opening of *The Wreck of the Deutschland*. The development of Brown's lyric verse is a development toward more clear opposition and a development toward a clearer, more rational, and more persuasive voice to bring water back into the channel again. What causes the pain, the twentieth-century reader asks? Is it the new science, the progress of technology, the loss of friends, the disappointment in hope that cut off the stream? A confessional poem — as twentieth-century writers have discovered — must confess all.

The 1868 poems repeatedly connect the speaking voice to dead and lifeless objects. In "The Pitcher" the speaker is compared to a dry channel. In "The Empty Cup" he is compared to a stone. In "A Morning Walk" the speaker is an aged man. Sand, weeds, and pebbles belong to the voice in "Triton Esuriens." In "Israel and Hellas" the voice is compared to a miserable, animal-like slave, in "Dreams" to a mummy. As a composite, the voice is the Dead King of the Wasteland. Not surprisingly, many of the poems employ a counter-metaphor of water to speak of the lamented regeneration that can not come. The promise is known, but the landscape is bare and speakers, as in "Alma Mater," orphaned.

"The Schooner" (October, 1868) dramatizes separation in a different way. It opens — as Brown's fine poems often do — with a sharp, clear picture. From a point on the land, a speaker describes a schooner "lying hoggish at the quay." Its sailors

> ...tugged, and stamped, and shoved, and pushed, and swore,
> And ever and anon, with crapulous glee,
> Grinned homage to viragoes on the shore.   (II, 348)

A sailor curses the harbor master. The ship is rotten from "gunwale to the keel, / Rat-riddled, bilge-bestank, / Slime-slobbered." The clot of words makes one think of Hopkins's poetry. Once at sea, the ship and its cursing, vulgar crew are transformed. At sea it is "a shadow of repose."

> So [the ship] sleeps, and dreams away,
> Soft-blended in a unity of rest
> All jars, and strifes obscene, and turbulent throes
> 'Neath the broad benediction of the West.   (II, 349)

Now the ship is "a spirit pure" ready to enter "Heaven's dockyard." The speaker is perfectly aware of the delusion; he knows the ship *is* the stinking, rotten object transformed by perspective. The speaker says, "methinks she changes as she sleeps" and the word *methinks,* so cloyed with use, perfectly qualifies the delusion. How pleasant if ugliness could be transcended by the simple expedient of perspective and a "methinks." The dirty ship is clear; the imagined ship is a dream. The reader detects the discrepancy between the grotesque reality and the equally grotesque dream.

"Israel and Hellas" (June, 1868) is much less overtly grotesque, but at every moment the idea of the poem threatens to turn into something else than its appearance in the poem. The poem shortly precedes the publication of Matthew Arnold's "Hebraism and Hellenism," one of the chapters of *Culture and Anarchy* then appearing in contemporary journals.[3] Brown repeats the Arnoldian point about the certainty and singleness of the well-lived life and echoes Arnold's line about the Greek "Who saw life steadily and saw it whole."[4] The speaker wonders if Greek life was as steady and firm as Greek buildings and words, or is Greek life, like the distant ship, attractive and calm only because it is distant? If Brown had possessed a time-machine, would he find the ancient world also rotten and bilge-bestank? The strangeness of the poem is the strangeness suggested by the intrusion of modern feeling on the ancient world. Brown is even more explicit when he places the moving, shifting values disturbing the present onto his imagined Greece:

> Or were they happier, breathing social free,
>   No smug respectability to pat
> And soothe with pledges of equality,
>   Ironical, whereat
> The goodman glows through all his realms of fat. (II, 378)

The repose of the sedate Victorian philistine is as vivid at the stinking schooner in harbor. The short fourth line ("Ironical, whereat") displays the complaisant vulgarity of the philistine in "all his realms of fat."

In the second half of this poem Brown imagines a "swart Hebrew with fiery haste" who comes to entwine Euphrosyne "In long brown arms." Brown quickly characterizes the Israel part of his title as if he were afraid of the "deep questionings [and] the deep replies." Having balanced Israel and Hellas, Brown manages to make the final verse, for once, steady and sure. Closure is his most difficult problem, and this one succeeds despite the faltering of two separate extra syllables in the line. If he were writing dialect, Brown would simply use apostrophes for the dropped syllables. In the English poem he has to rely on the beat of the line to place the emphasis.

> Yet, if the Greek went straighter to his aim,
>   If, knowing wholly what he meant to do,
> He did it, given circumstance the same,
>   Or near the same, then must I hold it true
> That from his different creed the vantage came,
>   Who, seizing one world where we balance two,
> From its great secular breast the readier current drew.
>
> (II, 379)

The words *secular* and *readier* fit awkwardly into the line. Even Arnold, for all his admiration of the Greeks, never dared such a conclusion: the Greek is admired because he seized *one* world. What were once "gleams upon the wave,/Long shafts that search the hearts of men who crave"[5] we have transformed, because of our duality, into "smug respectability" and "realms of fat." The steady line of Greek thinking has been bound by a "Nessus-robe, that may not be displaced" from Greek thought. Few others in 1868 could so fully opt for the single, secular Greek life.

Another poem, "Wastwater to Scafell" (1868), also poses two seeming balances that keep skewing off at an odd angle. The voice speaking the poem is that of Wast Water (as the Lake District map prints the name of the lake) speaking to Sca Fell, the 3200-foot peak that towers over it. The voice of the lake is thoroughly feminized. In the opening stanza, the lake kisses the mountain's feet, and speaks of the mountain as being "big and brave," "beautiful and strong," a woman's words for a man. The second stanza uses language appropriate to describe orgasm:

> Bare-breasted to the blast,
> Thou art at grips with him
> Steadfast, yet through each awful limb
> I feel the rock-veins start,
> And muscular thrillings darkly passed,
> And rigid throes, and a pulsation dim,
> And all the workings of thy heart. (I, 51)

Later the lake desires to enclose and absorb the mountain:

> But O, if thou couldst glide
> Into my arms, how I would pour
> Around thee sleeping, side, and breast, and brow —
> Storm-furrowed brow, and breast, and side!   (I, 52)

These words follow a section recalling the platonic love myth that lovers were once part of one whole and seek to be reunited. Even without modern psychiatry, we recognize that Brown means something by his masculine mountains and his feminine lake. The lake, speaking throughout the poem, imagines a union, and the language becomes incantatory:

> I would bind thee every way —
> O! I'd crown thee, and I'd drown thee,
> And I'd bathe thee, and I'd swathe thee
> With the swirling and the curling,
> And the splashing and the flashing
> Of my arms. (I, 52)

The speaking lake, however, recognizes that this union is only a dream. "[We] must obey, / Nor move but with the moving sphere" of "The ordered world." No matter how much desired, how much dreamed of, we have to be content to "joy and grieve." The poem makes concrete the pain of separation, of eternal duality. These lovers can never join.

The earliest written of Brown's published poems contains the same violent disunion. The poem is entitled "Hotwells" but nothing in it suggests what the name means. A Manx critic reports that the poem is named for "one of the most immoral districts of Bristol."[6] In the poem a lover speaks about a woman whom he sees again after a long absence. She has "dull stony eyes" in a face that "used to light with meek surprise." Once the speaker praised her beauty. Now, however, she is a "fearful thing of Hell."

Here the balance between opposites is resolved, but it is done violently. The love of the man has now turned into hate for the mask "carved rigid on the shell":

> Yet, if the soul remain,
> There crouched and dumb behind the obdurate mask,
> This would I ask: —
> Kill her, O God! that so, the flesh being slain,
> Her soul my soul may be again.   (I, 70)

The editors of the Golden Treasury anthology of Brown's poems print a letter which accompanied the poem when it was written on June 8, 1868:

I sometimes write little things at night. It would be so delightful, at least so soothing, if we both did, and exchanged, just to show that our souls live. As an experiment, I send you this. The lines were suggested by a woman I saw in the Hotwells this morning.[7]

What could be soothing about writing such a poem? The key phrase in the letter seems to be "that our souls live." Is the fact of feeling itself in the poem the necessary anodyne? John Stuart Mill in his *Autobiography* says that he began to emerge from his great despair in 1828 when he shed spontaneous tears on reading the description of a dying parent. Possibly Brown means to say that the emotion, the feeling, no matter how strange, is sufficient in this dry land. The letter and the poem suggest that in 1868 Brown felt himself so divided that only by such a violent yoking could he bring a sense of reality back into his life.

II *Existence and Dream*

Two poems of 1869, "Clifton" and "Epistola ad Dakyns,"
bear further testimony to the split in Brown's life between the fact
of existence and the possibility of dream. "Clifton" was modified
for its 1893 publication in *Old John,* but originally it marked
Brown's sixth year at Clifton College. It is a schizophrenic poem
because it so perfectly divides life between dull, predictable Clifton
and the wild freedom of an imagined life on the Isle of Man. In
Freud's terms *pleasure* and *reality,* the poem contrasts the reality of
social order at Clifton against the pleasure of freedom on the removed island. The poem says, I can bear my isolation because I
dream of the freedom of Scarlett Rocks, Barrule, and Bradda (all
scenic places on the Isle of Man). The poem, therefore, signals
Brown's escape to the Isle of Man of the imagination and signals
his writing the Anglo-Manx narratives.

The "Epistola ad Dakyns" is, curiously enough, a self-elegy. It
imagines that Brown is dead, and he tells his friend Hugh Graham
Dakyns where he could go to discover what Brown "*meant, not
did.*" His spirit will haunt three places — the banks of the Avon at
Clifton, the Lake District, and the Isle of Man. After death Brown
has found union, become incorporate, with these places. To look
back to "Hotwells" for a moment, he seems to say that once his
own obdurate mask is destroyed by death, his soul may be joined
with the beloved again. When Dakyns goes to the banks of the
Avon, he will feel there "A spirit with a spirit blended,... / A
wraith, a film, a memory" (II, 364). In the Lake District "Where
Derwent ... gives her bosom to the skies" (II, 364), Dakyns will
feel "a quickening pulse in earth and sky, / And you shall know
that it is I" (II, 365). On the Isle of Man he will find his essence
"wedded to those primal forms" (II, 366). He imagines himself

> Sphered in the very heart of it [the island].
> And every hill from me shall shoot,
> And spread as from a central root...
> And I shall be the living heart,
> And I shall live in every part.   (II, 366)

In death, the pitcher will then be full, the waters will flow in desert
places. The schooner will reach perfection in the distance; the water
of the lake will be joined to the flesh of the mountain. In his own
elegy, written when he was thirty-nine, Brown discovers how the

anguish of his life can be "soothed" by the thought of soul union
to a landscape.

Brown achieves his union by a curious and intense identification
with places and objects in the world. His own living, suffering spirit
will somehow escape from his body to enter places on the Isle of
Man in "Clifton" and places in England, the Lake District, and the
Isle of Man again in "Epistola." TEB reverses primitive animism
which imagines that the world's objects have souls; in TEB, his
spirit and soul project into the world. The voice in these poems
seems desperate, anxious, insecure, double. Existence is irritating;
"the truculent quack / Insists with acrid shriek my ears to prod,"
he writes in "Clifton." Against these others, these quacks, TEB's
poems have the dream of merging into a landscape.

"Clifton" and "Epistola ad Dakyns," two simple-seeming
poems, repeat the yearning, anguished ideas of other early poems.
The grotesque and bizarre are modified in these poems, but still
they reveal an anguished and pained soul seeking a unity it can
hardly know.

III   *Beyond Laughter*

In 1869 TEB wrote eighteen lyric poems; in the five years from
1870–75, he wrote only four. He was writing his poems in Manx
dialect. The next dated English poems were written for *Plain Talk,*
the periodical of the Baptist congregation where Hugh Stowell
Brown preached God's word to the working men of Liverpool.
Thomas Edward Brown would write very plainly to suit the readers
of *Plain Talk*. His audience was not the audience to which English
poetry had been addressed in any previous time, but city "folk" of
a new industrial age. The poems all have a heavy obviousness about
them. Brown never lets his clear, direct pictures stand. The poems
of 1868 have drama; the *Plain Talk* poems make simple statements
about unions. The opposition seems resolved, but of course it is
not.

TEB published fourteen of the nineteen poems written in 1875 in
Plain Talk. The first poem is typical of the whole group. "Indwell-
ing" (titled in 1875 "No Room" and not signed) speaks about a
soul emptying itself so that God may fill the space; if God finds the
body full of self and activity, He judges there is "no room" for
Him. His earlier poem, "The Pitcher" (1868) was about an empty
soul that despaired of ever being full. Brown merely turned his old

poem around and made it a versified pious thought. "Preparations" (1875) says each man is like a musical instrument that must be kept in tune so that God may play it; "Planting" (1875) says that man should expect to be planted and grow like the lilies of the field. In the *Plain Talk* poems, thought is perfectly sincere, perfectly safe, and perfectly clear. H. Stowell Brown had no interest in poetry, and the verse TEB sent him is not poetry.

TEB's best-known poem, "My Garden" (1876), was first published in *Plain Talk*. Sir Arthur Quiller-Couch placed it as the final poem in one edition of his *Oxford Book of English Verse;* thus English literature moved from "The Seafarer" to "My Garden," from heroic adventure to a pleasant conceit fit to be placed in a suburban garden. The irony was too obvious; further, TEB's words and rhymes invite merciless parody. The poem ought to have died quietly in the files of an obscure parish magazine, and yet even here Brown is softening down what has been violent and energetic in other early poems. The text is short enough so that the whole poem may be printed once again:

> A garden is a lovesome thing, God wot!
> Rose plot,
> Fringed pool,
> Ferned grot —
> The veriest school
> Of peace; and yet the fool
> Contends that God is not—
> Not God! in gardens! when the eve is cool!
> Nay, but I have a sign;
> 'Tis very sure God walks in mine.

Again TEB projects a spirit into a landscape, but now he projects by mere statement rather than dramatic exploration of division. The separation exists — else why call the other man a fool? — and still haunts the speaker.

Many a bright young man in the twentieth century has had fun with "My Garden" (A garden is a gruesome thing), but TEB, knowing his Baptist audience, wrote to please that audience. His success is testified whenever we see the words tacked up in a suburban garden. "My Garden" seems to us a cultural expression so appallingly bad and apparent that finally we begin to see genius in its total banality, its total realization of itself. The urban "folk" of H. Stowell Brown's Baptist chapel probably loved the poem. Even in the late twentieth century, it keeps TEB's memory alive: mention Brown's name to readers of verse and one is apt to hear words about "What rot, God wot." The reader of all TEB's verse may prefer the poems with more dramatic duality, but Brown in "My Garden" attained a kind of perfect simplicity that is memorable. The poem — one regrets to say — lodged in the language.

Other poems of 1875, however, return to the painful dichotomy or duality of Brown's earliest poems. These have a serious success, but they require much more attention and care in reading than "My Garden." "Risus Dei" (1875), for example, explores the meaning of laughter. The nineteenth century was uneasy with laughter. A sure way for a writer to lose his reputation was to write comic verse; a great deal of it, however, was written and enjoyed. Victorians preferred comic poems "that did not really mean anything."[8] Brown, who by 1875 had begun to write comic Manx poems, is justifying himself. Laughter is a "Godlike function." Laughter protects fools; it inhabits "a sacred core of sadness." Even the devil has the right to laughter. The poem ends with the recognition that no matter where a man goes to laugh, be it the highest peak of a cliff, a nearby shepherd lad will "deem that you were mad." The comic and the serious, the sane and the mad, exist in the same painful opposition as Brown's earlier yokings. He will attempt the subject of laughter in a later poem on a Manx fool, "Chalse A Killey." He finds other dualities in "Reconciliation" (1875), a poem that apparently starts as a landscape picture in Brown's best manner. He seems to be describing two hills. Suddenly the poem shifts to talk about brothers who are as separate as hills across a narrow valley. One thinks immediately of his brother H. Stowell Brown, who so radically differed from TEB. In "The Dhoon" (1875) Brown brings back the male-female contrast of "Wastwater to Scafell." This time he writes about a Manx stream, the masculine figure, that flows down toward the ocean, the receiving female. The unity of opposites occurs when one disappears.

"Chalse A Killey" (1875) may have been published during the year of composition on the Isle of Man.[9] It should have been read and attended to by both Manxmen and Englishmen. Unlike the *Plain Talk* platitudes, this poem has an antic, nervous energy. It tries an unusual subject and it releases strange energies. Chalse was a mad wanderer on the Isle of Man whom Brown had known at Archdeacon Moore's rectory in Andreas. Both TEB and Chalse had been quondam sons of Moore. From a simple figure of mem-

ory, Chalse turns into a specter, some ghost of the imagination that
is more than memory. Chalse may be TEB.

The poem opens with Chalse dead. Almost immediately the
reader senses that "Chalse A Killey" describes not so much Chalse
as Brown himself in the anguished, uncertain 1868 poems:

> And now it's all so plain, dear Chalse!
> So plain—
> The wildered brain,
> The joy, the pain —
> The phantom shapes that haunted,
> The half-born thoughts that daunted —
> All, all, is plain
> Dear Chalse!
> All is plain.   (I, 12–13)

The repeated "All is plain" only convinces the reader that all is in
fact not plain at all. Brown, in his description of Chalse, repeats the
same contrast between duty and release in a landscape that he had
used in "Clifton" and the "Epistola ad Dakyns." Chalse wonders
if, in discovering surcease from his pain, he has to lose the "memory / Of land and sea," the "gleams" on the mountain Barrule,
and the "soft wind" of the Curraghs (the swampy plain at the
northern extremity of the island). Possibly he can give up the
mountains if now he has "pierced through the veiled delusions, /
The errors and confusions" of ordinary mortal life.

Chalse, even in madness, has made music. Surely heaven will
find use for him. The speaker recalls Chalse helping Parson Drury
"put the *Romans* out," Chalse preaching to the children at Rushen
when the Parson was gone, and finally Chalse preaching to three
painters and himself on the evils of drink. An empty bottle in his
hand serves for a "palpable typology." In recalling the memories,
the speaker's tone changes from the simple comedy of the first
presentation to the pathos of the final scene:

> Dear Chalse, you never had
> An audience more silent or more sad!   (I, 15)

Brown keeps the poem tart, however, by a picture of Chalse setting
up his hymns on a heavenly press,

> Founded with gems

Of living sapphire, dipped
In blood of molten rubies, diamond-tipped.   (I, 15)

And thus his songs are distributed.

The poem acquires a special ambiance when we recall that it was written in 1875. Brown had written by that time at least four dialect poems. Only one of these poems had been published off the Isle of Man, and then it was published in a reduced version. In 1875, he began to write again in standard English rather than dialect. Brown must have felt in a position analogous to that of Chalse A Killey, a madman telling tales in a dialect that no one understood. Chalse A Killey was funny; Brown was funny. As "The ways were cold, the ways were rough" to Chalse, they were cold and rough to Brown. Chalse's soul was dark; the voice of the 1868 poems complains that its soul too is dark. When Brown suggests that Chalse will get his songs printed in heaven, he hints that perhaps he too might have to wait to get his poems published in heaven. The poem, however, is nervous and tense; are we to laugh at the simple fool or are we to respect him? Is he simply mad or is his madness the divine madness? Are we to lament his death or be grateful that death has released such a soul to more ample realms?

The poems published in Hugh Stowell Brown's *Plain Talk* would never be taken to be madness or foolish; yet they seem such limp exercises on tired conventions that they could represent a kind of madness of perfect conformity. "Chalse A Killey" is the antitype of the *Plain Talk* poems. Brown's personal anguish has found a dramatic expression. The poem presents a curious, disturbing, ambiguous human being. That nineteenth-century drive for a poetry of feeling (against the versified prose of thought in the eighteenth century) suddenly succeeds. The writer has moved his reader from observation of a particular man to an observation of the precarious condition of human intelligence. That we are frightened, disturbed, and moved by the experience testifies to the power of the poem.

IV   *Death and Women*

After 1875 Brown's lyric impulse was dominated by death. In 1875 his mother died. In the spring of 1876, his seven-year-old son Braddan died of diphtheria. In 1882 one brother died; in 1886 another. In the 1880s his close friend James Maurice Wilson's wife died and Wilson's son fell to his death from a cliff near Bristol. Brown wrote about mining disasters and ships sinking. He even wrote an obituary poem for a man who had said he had enjoyed "Chalse A Killey." Brown repeatedly confessed that he had no equipment to understand these separations. When he thought that kings and chimney sweeps come to dust, he shuddered. The poems ruminate and meditate, and, like Miniver Cheevy, curse the day of human birth.

"Aber Stations" (1879), on the death of his son Braddan, is typical. Four years before Brown had visited the falls near Llanfairfechan in Wales with his then six-year-old son. In each of the seven places where they went, and where the father now returns, some aspect of the dead son's character is invoked. The poem is moving, but the feeling is that of an absolutely exposed nerve ending. The poem is the nadir of one artistic idea. Its confession is extreme, complete, and naked. Brown's voice, so damaged by his loss, finally can do nothing but cry. Brown said that his father was a "born sobber"; in this poem he too sobs. In periods when the artistic aim is to be natural, real, or honest, Brown's poem on his dead son will find readers; in periods when the artistic mode aims at formal design with detached control of emotions, the poem fails. One can imagine Ezra Pound reading "Aber Stations" and shouting in fury.

The poem moves rapidly, and Brown uses sharp, clear detail; the boisterous sound of an English blackbird, a piece of grit on the pathway, and the memory of the once-lively boy come together in a vivid picture that John Millais or Edward Burne-Jones might have painted. The speaker recalls that the boy walked where the blackbird now is singing, and wonders where the boy's foot is now.

> a fascicle
> Of crumbling bones
> Jammed in with earth and stones.
> You say that this is old,
> A tale twice-told —
> Say what you will:
> Old, new, I swear
> That it is horrible —
> Horrible, blackbird, howsoe'er
> The Spring rejoices you with its budding bloom —
> Yes, horrible, most horrible!
> Though you should carol to the crack of doom,
> Poor blackbird! being so absolutely glad.   (II, 354)

The painters would have enjoyed contrasting the bird, the pathway where the father walks, and the six-year-old dream-child walking in the Welsh mountains. Like the pictures, the poem's lushness, detail, and sentiment characterize the age.

Like "Chalse A Killey" three years before, "Catherine Kinrade" (1878) utilizes a Manx story and setting. Catherine is an historical figure. In 1713 and 1720 Bishop Thomas Wilson punished Catherine for her four illegitimate children. To bring her to "a timely and thorough reformation" (I, 43–44), as the historical data that Brown prefixes to his poem have it, Catherine was dragged around Peel Harbour behind a boat. Catherine, according to the Bishop, was a notorious strumpet, leading "a most vicious and scandalous life." After being dragged behind the boat a second time and forced to "perform public penance in all the churches of this island," she is (the Bishop finally certifies) "according to her capacity" now qualified "to be received into the peace of the Church." Her separate realities — to use Brown's trope — have been yoked together.

Brown's poem imagines the good Bishop — acknowledged to be the best ever to head the Manx See — entering heaven only to discover that Catherine Kinrade is already "divinely clothed in white" with her four cherubs. The Bishop mistakes her for Christ's mother. The poem continues by contrasting the Bishop's last sight of her, "God's image trodden in the mire . . . by no fault of hers," with the present sight when

> some vital spring adjusted,
> Some faculty that rusted
> Cleansed to legitimate use. . . .
>   No more
> In that dark grave entombed
> Her soul had bloomed
> To perfect woman.   (I, 45)

The poem ends with Catherine kissing the Bishop and all reconciled. The poem might be described as "a pretty piece of piety" and, like his earlier poem "Hotwells," one more example of Brown's pained awareness of the fallen condition. Unlike "Hotwells," which demanded that God kill the body so that the soul could remain, Catherine Kinrade is now a pure soul whose purity condemns the Bishop who tried to reform her.

The women in "Roman Women" are, like Catherine Kinrade, all

much too sexually alive for bishops and Englishmen. Brown worked on "Roman Women" in 1895 and published it in the *New Review* for August, 1895, but his own manuscript carries the date "Rome, 1879–80, Dec.-Jan."[10] The vigorous sexuality of the poem leads me to believe that it was finished in 1879–80 and, like "Wastwater to Scafell," omitted from *Old John* in expectation that the Macmillan editors would not appreciate the frank, open sexuality of its various pictures. In all, there are fourteen sections of the poem, each a portrait of a woman. The first thirteen are Romans, but the last is an Englishwoman whom the speaker sees on the Pincian Hill. He opposes the Englishwoman, dead in life, to all the warm, live Roman women. One of the women, with two "great eyes, . . . sucked me down the Maelstrom of her heart." Another woman is "round-ribbed, large-flanked / Broad-shouldered." Another is a "Good wife, good mother" who seems fit "to hold Jove's offspring on her knees" (I, 57–58). In the ninth poem of the sequence a passing face interests a British tourist more than the Forum of Augustus. In the tenth poem, the Englishman asks a Roman woman to blow in his ears,

> Blow *in* the cooing of the dove,
> Blow *out* the singing of the salt!   (I, 59)

One of the most interesting lines is spoken by an Italian girl visiting St. Peter's who remembers a "hungry Englishman" watching her "as if he'd eat her."

Balanced against these warm, glowing women is the final poem describing the "Englishwoman on the Pincian" who is as cold as the Italian women are warm:

> I know your mechanism well-adjusted,
> I see your mind and body have been trusted,
> To all the proper people.   (I, 60)

She knows the use of soap-and-water, but the speaker could never love her. She has virtues; she has gone to the "desolate and grim" northern landscapes. He knows how

> the progress of our civilisation
> Has made you quite so terrible. . .
>   still
> You have us stalwart scions,

> Suckled the young sea lions,
> And smiled infrequent, glacial smiles
> Upon the sulky isles.   (I, 62)

She belongs at home away from the "passion-flowers" and "sunny hours."

In a terrible sense, it is a voyeur's poem; the speaker looks and looks ("just as if he'd eat her"), but nothing happens. Despite its lustiness, it is detached. The speaker yearns for the warmth, but he knows the coldness of the Englishwoman. The futility of the desire testifies, however, to the strength of desire. The special case of sexual loneliness in the poems is part of the larger isolation and death that the speaking voice in Brown's verse repeatedly attests to.

Among the undated twenty-eight poems (out of a total of some one hundred and twenty) two are particularly striking: "Nature and Art" and "Dartmoor: Sunset at Chagford." Both poems attack large questions with wit and each has balanced, opposed parts. Thus the divided soul is visible, part of the structure of the poem.

In the first section of "Nature and Art" a somewhat sappy Victorian voice discovers that nature is not a paraclete but is in fact neutral:

> It is because thou seem'st at our alarms
>   Unmoved: the ages fall
> Helpless from out the rigour of thine arms,
>   Thou heeding not at all
>   If the bridal veil or pall
> Bedeck thine immortality of charms.[11]

Possibly we are so alienated from this neutral Nature because a foster-sister, Art, has created a new dimension and reality.

After the lugubrious first voice, Art in the second part speaks in a much lustier tone. In the opening lines of the second half, Art herself replies:

> O Heaven! the puppy! Is this gratitude?
>   "A Foster-sister" saidst thou?
> An "Art of Life"? What fell Locusta stewed
>   That damned Fucus? Spreads thou
>   That unction on thy soulcule? Wed'st thou

That specious harlotry from hell's black bosom spewed?[12]
(*Fucus*: obs. a face paint
Soulcule: a little soul [his invention])

Art speaks as if slightly drunk. She repeats the subjects of anguish and passion, but all in the tone of "Don't be such a silly: acquire some sense of proportion." The poem satirizes the cherished Victorian image of the soul lost in nature "red in tooth and claw," but it also concludes that nature and art are "Both wrong, both right." Presumably a third thing in "the wills of men" keeps these oppo-sites in harmony. The poem, after long sections on each error, does not resolve itself satisfactorily. The speaking voice cannot yoke, cannot resolve, the opposites.

Brown solves the problem of closure, however, in "Dartmoor: Sunset at Chagford" (n.d.) since he wisely allows his two voices to rest without final comment. The editors of the *Collected Poems,* where the poem was first published, gave the title "Homo Loqui-tur" (Man speaking) to the first section to parallel Brown's title "Respondet Demiurgus" (the secondary deity responds) for the second part.[13] Man denies the power of sunsets; they are "a mam-moth joke," the garbage of the gods. If sunsets are the food of gods, he will have none, but he does suspect that sunsets come from the cloaca of heaven. He means *cloaca*, the intestinal tract of birds and reptiles, and thus sunsets are a kind of excrement. The image is Swiftian in its audacity. Man wants no anodyne or opiate to dull his agony:

> I will not be put off with temporal pretence:
> I want to be awake, and know, not stand
> And stare at waving of a conjuror's hand.   (II, 334)

As the speaker in "Nature and Art," this speaker knows that sun-sets are neutral; the colors go to "the virgin chaste" and "in a harlot's eyes," to blades of grass and spiders "in their foul pavilions." This meaning of nature is, to all eyes, unclear.

> The leech
> Looks from its muddy lair,
> And sees a silly something in the air—
> Call you this *speech*?
> Speak plainer. (II, 336)

If nature is a language, it is painfully obscure.

The speaker has another thought that is almost metaphysical in its audacity. If man spends life receiving sense data, possibly in some heavenly dissection room, God and his angels open skulls to study the data received. Brown's speaker plays out the fancy. God and the angels find the smoky yellow of one sunset, and the filmy pink of that other one. After thanking an angel who has delivered a lancet, God notices one particular sunset that is Manx:

> Another lancet — thanks!
> That's Manx —
> Yes, the delicate pale sea-green
> Passing into ultra-marine —
> A little blurred — in fact
> This brain seems packed
> With sunsets.   (II, 336–37)

The bizarre picture of the dissection room controls the tone so that we don't feel we have another romantic gushing over

> the gleam,
> The light that never was, on sea or land,
> The consecration, and the Poet's dream.[14]

Those words belong to Wordsworth not Brown, but Wordsworth lived in an earlier time; Brown needs his mad astringency to examine once more the notion that the brain is a storehouse for sunsets, for memory, and for experience.

In the second half of the poem Demiurgus answers. He does his work of creating; he obeys his own laws and persists because he must. He has no speech for man; he is no surgeon with a lancet who can dissect the brain. He simply provides joys.

> What
> And what if I impart
> The same to frog or newt,
> What if I steep the root
> Of some old stump in bright vermilion,
> And if the spider in his quaint pavilion
> Catches a sunbeam where he thought a fly?   (II, 339)

The tone is colloquial, detached, objective — almost relaxed and easy.

In the last lines, the tone becomes even more colloquial as Demiurgus explains,

> You see, I am a servant, that is it:
> You've hit
> The mark — a servant; for the other word —
> Why, you are Lord, if any one is lord.   (II, 340)

The real power in the universe is human perception. Consciousness,
the awareness of sunsets, is the divinity. Thus Brown arrives, on his
own route, at a resolution much like his contemporaries'. They all
start with the simple facts of their own feelings as sufficient evidence of something larger than themselves. If we feel and remember pain, then we are more than beasts. The something out there
not ourselves (as Arnold defined God) becomes something in ourselves that imagines, appreciates, and enjoys. Brown did not seize
this perception and ride off triumphantly with it as W. B. Yeats did.
In his English lyrics he captures only sporadically the sense of realization, the resolution of his violent oppositions. He wraps the
resolution in comedy or in the grotesque (sunsets as heavenly excrement). "Dartmoor" does succeed; it should lodge as firmly in the
language as "My Garden."

In 1965, Ramsey Moore read "Dartmoor" aloud to persons
interested in Brown's verse and in his reputation. Moore was
Attorney-General of the Isle of Man and author of the "Introduction" to the 1930 *Memorial Volume.* He may have been the instiga-
tor. When he finished reading, moved by the poem and its ending,
he said, "This proves he could have been a classical English poet.
Instead, he sacrificed himself to the Manx." Moore wished for
more poems like "Dartmoor," and any reader would share the
desire with him. In his Manx poems, however, TEB achieved more
consistently this vision that is only fitful in the English lyrics.

Brown claimed in 1868 that he wrote to "soothe" himself and to
convince himself that in the great dualities, the great oppositions,
the great contrasts, his soul was not dead but alive. The Roman
women have this life. If neither god nor nature supplies easy and
satisfactory answers for life questions, then the sheer awareness of
life forces may substitute. Most of Brown's mainstream English
critics agree with Ramsey Moore that Brown's literary "merit must
rest ... on the lyrics."[15] The poems do have merit. The best create
vivid scenes and images like that in "The Schooner," where a busy,

greasy, provincial harbor is fully realized. "Roman Women" has fine energy and salty intelligence.

In two other poems written in the late 1870s, Brown resolved the dualities of speech and nationality and, as in "Dartmoor," found faith in vision, and both of these poems have Manx settings. In "Chalse A Killey," TEB speculated on the meaning of mad, comic speech, and in "Catherine Kinrade," he speculated on foreign bishops imposing harsh moral codes on living people. In "Braddan Vicarage" (1877) and "Old John" (1880), he returned to Man to find stability in "life's grave complexity" ("Old John").

Brown grew up at Braddan Vicarage, and in the first thirteen stanzas, of his poem of that name, twelve of them beginning, "I wonder," he imagines another boy growing up on the Isle of Man and becoming aware first of sky, then sycamore, ash, the sea-blast, the flowers, and the mountains. Off to the East the boy will catch faint gleams "where Cumbria looms a geographic ghost." On a clear day, one can see the coast of Cumberland in England from the Isle of Man. The more evident presence to the boy, however, is the English captain "from the proud East," a man with a horny hand, "Who swears the mighty oath" and holds "serene command" of his ship. Beginning as an idyl of childhood, the poem suddenly turns again toward that duality of all the poems here discussed. How is the child to view the English? Are they "A higher type beyond his reach, / Imperial blood, by Heaven ordained with pen / And sword"? Is the boy awed when he "hears the tones as of an alien speech"? The boy may suspect they are "a braggart race," who have "technic skill and aim, / And all the prosperous fraud that binds their social frame." The young rebel "knows not what / He hates, yet hates." The final stanza, however, says that rebellion is crude and undisciplined, that the boy should rather, "keep the larger equipoise, / And stand outside these nations and their noise." In short, TEB advises a new young Manxman to be himself rather than to be awed or angry about the "land of Edwards and of Henries." Brown's sense is clear enough. His persona is drawn and repulsed by England, its land, and its history. Every colonial feels the same attraction and repulsion, but he must also know (as the final stanza suggests) that it is precisely this attraction and repulsion that make him a colonial.

The poem "Old John" (1880) celebrates the Scots servant who was more of a father than TEB's natural father, but this man is not "of our church, nor of our speech." Old John was TEB's boy-

hood teacher and, Scots Methodist though he was, his priest. It is a
long poem of thirty-five stanzas, each seven and one-half lines
long. It is also a comic poem. TEB tells of overhearing Old John
praying for the troubled Brown family:

> your groans and sighs
> And grasps I heard by listening at the gable,
> Inside of which you knelt, and shook the skies—
> But first the stable.   (I, 7)

Old John taught TEB and his brothers how to stack hay and how to
identify birds (the lines are in mock Miltonics). He told stories
about Scotland; Old John talked to the boy "Of God, and faith,
and hope, / And resurrection." He taught the boy "to look beyond
convention's frimsy trammel." The poem ends with a genre picture
of a scene that took place between 1846 and 1850 when TEB no longer lived at Braddan Vicarage. TEB has returned for a visit but
stays too late; he sleeps overnight with Old John and next morning
breakfasts with the family. The poem concludes,

> O faithfullest! my debt to you is long;
> Life's grave complexity around me grows.
> From you it comes if in the busy throng
> Some friends I have, and have not any foes;
> And even now, when purple morning glows,
> And I am on the hills, a night-worn watchman,
> I see you in the centre of the rose,
> Dear, brave, old Scotchman.   (I, 12)

Despite Old John's language — the poem has fun with his Scots
pronunciations — the old man (seventy-five in 1847) understood
his world. He has reached that unity and understanding that TEB
himself sought in his other English lyrics. In the comic mode, TEB
speaks more fully and completely than in many of his English
lyrics, where the comedy is intermittent. Old John's Scots speech is
mad and funny, but it is true. In "Chalse A Killey," TEB talks
about Chalse's madness and comedy as "that crazed instrument /
That God had given you here for use" (I, 13). Brown himself had
in the Manx dialect a "crazed instrument," both broken and
comic, that was his gift. Only sporadic in the English poems, the
comedy is consistent and dramatic in his Manx narratives. He
might have been a classical English poet, but he is more interesting

when he sacrificed himself for the Manx. In the "wildered brain" of his Manx poems, the opposition of "joy and pain" ("Chalse") resolve consistently into pure vision, bringing joy and pain into one.

CHAPTER 7

On Publishing a Victorian Epic:
Fo'c's'le Yarns: First Series

"O, it's very shockin'! it's very shockin'!"
"What's shockin'?" I says. "O," he says, "it's no use
Pretendin', young man!" "Well, why the deuce,"
Says I, "can't you give the thing a name?"
"O, raely!" says he, "for shame! for shame!"

"Betsy Lee," *Poems,* I, 113.

THERE is nothing so exciting and so awe-inspiring in the world
of letters as the spectacle of a great spirit daring to risk everything on one great venture and knowing that in its execution he will
be taxed to the limit of what a man can endure,"[1] wrote E. M. W.
Tillyard in *The English Epic and Its Background.* Tillyard's history
of the epic stops at the end of the eighteenth century. After that
time, the effort to subsume life in one vision became chiefly the
business of the novelist. The nineteenth century had long poems —
Wordsworth's *Prelude,* Shelley's *Prometheus Unbound,* Byron's
Don Juan, Browning's *Ring and the Book,* and Hardy's *Dynasts* —
but in no case did the writer risk everything on a single vision.
Thomas Edward Brown attempted just that single venture:

> To sing a song shall please my countrymen;
> To unlock the treasures of the Island heart;
> With loving feet to trace each hill and glen,
> . . .
> . . . for mine own people do I sing,
> And use the old familiar speech:
> Happy if I shall reach
> Their inmost consciousness.[2]

He made his effort in twelve narrative poems, *Fo'c's'le Yarns*. Ten of the poems are spoken by Tom Baynes, a Manx sailor, in the crew's quarters of a ship at sea. An eleventh story, "Mary Quayle," is spoken in the voice of a Manx curate, and a twelfth, "Bella Gorry," is told by Parson Gale. The last two stories are in standard English, but the others are in a bounding, energetic, Anglo-Manx dialect, a supple tool that is marvelously inventive and alive. Brown restated his aim in the introductory poem:

> Dear countrymen, whate'er is left to us
>   Of ancient heritage —
> Of manners, speech, of humours, polity
> The limited horizon of our stage —
>   Old love, hope, fear,
>   All this I fain would fix upon the page;
>   That so the coming age,
>   Lost in the empire's mass,
>   Yet haply longing for their fathers, here
>   May see, as in a glass
>   What they held dear —
> May say, "'Twas thus and thus
>   They lived"; and, as the time-flood onward rolls,
>   Secure an anchor for their Keltic souls.[3]   (II, 1)

He sought, in short, to grasp a total way of life and give that life its full scope. He was taxed to the limit of endurance in his great aim.

The aim of the epic poet, as Tillyard paraphrases Milton's aim, is "to realise the potentiality of his vernacular."[4] Brown, however, was considerably restricted by his English publishers, who had ideas about what vernacular he should use. Five of Brown's poems exist in editions before their London publication and in every case his texts are mutilated in their later forms.

Brown wrote the first four narratives to be discussed here — "Betsy Lee," "Christmas Rose," "Captain Tom and Captain Hugh," and "Tommy Big-Eyes," — in the period 1870–75, completing the whole sequence and publishing it all by 1895. From the beginning he aimed to present the broad spectrum of Manx life which would enable him to realize the potentiality of the dialect. In the first four he writes about fishermen, farmers, sailors, and churchmen, both Methodist and Established Church. Two are set in the southern part of the island, one in the central, and one in the north. The main characters in these first four narratives come from the lower orders of society. Betsy Lee is the daughter of a fisherman who receives an inheritance which enables him to move to a small farm. Christmas Rose lives in the vicarage with Parson Gale and his family, clearly a major step up in the social ladder since, to their ruin, some of the persons have pretensions to gentility. Captain Tom and Captain Hugh are both ship captairis. "Tommy Big-Eyes" takes place on a large Manx farm in the northern reaches of the island, and Tommy becomes a successful merchant in Douglas, the capital. Because Tom Baynes' true love, Betsy Lee, dies in the first story, he is in all other stories a bachelor who loves from afar and who loves every heroine in the sequence. The subject in all the narratives is about a deep human love, passing all understanding. Some accident or fate bars union; lovers are as separate as Wast Water and Sca Fell in the lyric poems. Actual lovers often grow up in the same household or as near neighbors; Tom Baynes and Betsy Lee grow up as brother and sister; Christmas Rose is raised as the sister to George and James Gale who fall in love with her; the young lovers in "Captain Tom and Captain Hugh" are cousins raised in adjoining houses; Tommy Big-Eyes sets up housekeeping with his wife's mother. The Isle of Man is a small community; TEB married a second cousin. As in the English lyrics, the Manx narratives dream of an almost impossible union, a unity beyond ordinary experience. Brown's people are as isolated as Brown himself was at Oxford or at Clifton College.

In 1871 or 1872 TEB had a printer in Cockermouth, Lake District (Wordsworth's birthplace), run off copies of "Betsy Lee" on newsprint.[5] Wordsworth had said that the poet is nothing more than a man speaking to men, and Brown's poem seeks to be just that. Like all true epics, "Betsy Lee" needs to be read aloud. We don't have Brown's "mimetic force,"[6] or even that of his friend James Maurice Wilson, who knew "Betsy Lee's" fifteen hundred lines by heart and recited them on every occasion, the last time in 1930 at the centenary of Brown's birth when Wilson himself was nearly one hundred. Manxmen recite the poems at their national festivals. Non-Manx readers have to imagine the lilting Manx rhythms.

The bounding Manx vitality, however, had to be calmed and tamed before the poems could be published in London in 1881, some ten years after their composition. Brown himself cut the text on direction from his London publisher and clearly he did not approve what London demanded. As Brown says, the poems had to be emasculated:

Mr. [George Lillie] Craik wrote to me about my 'poemes'. I asked him to mark the passages that *bored* him as being tedious, superfluous and flat. No doubt he has been too busy to return the matter. Meantime I have been cutting out at a great rate. My poor Tom Baynes will now appear in the character of a castrato, more musical, I hope, certainly less formidable, and less vigorous. Somehow I don't seem to care much about him. Tom ought to swear, and that hugely — I have not left him a single oath: he ought to handle scripture with a fine freedom — I have stopped 'his allowance' of texts.

I don't know whether you are familiar with [George] Crabbe's *Tales:* there is one about a poor old sailor who gets 'done to death' by the gentility of an awful sister-in-law and the cowardice of a sneaking brother. My old salt is very nearly in the same case.[7]

Brown indicates the obvious changes he made in his text. Everytime Tom says *God* or *d*____ the words are eliminated and milder words inserted. He is even rationed on "My Gough," a mild Manx expletive, something like the American "My Gosh."

In 1888, when Macmillan was preparing a second edition of *Fo'c's'le Yarns,* Brown asked that the cuts be restored:

The first alteration I propose is in *Betsy Lee.* I wish to restore the original motive as given in your 1873 edition. I think this restoration is quite necessary. The toning down of this passage was due to a well-meant desire and a modest ambition to get *Betsy Lee* admitted as a "drawing-room book." This it signally failed to become, and it must steer out into the open sea of literature; let it wear its true colours.[8]

The cuts in "Betsy Lee" have never been restored. All critical comment on the poem uses the mutilated text. In February, 1897, Brown advised a reader to use the texts in the Isle of Man *Times* rather than the Macmillan text.[9] Brown's friends did not restore his texts for the *Collected Poems* (1900), and the 1952 Liverpool edition continues to print the disavowed text. Thus his narratives have not steered "out into the open sea of literature"; Tom Baynes is not allowed to "give the thing a name" (see verse at chapter opening).

I   *Rustic Love and London Publishers*

In "Betsy Lee" Tom Baynes is both narrator and principal actor. He tells the story to a group of skeptical fellow Manx in the foreward hold of a ship. In all but two of the stories, the vision is entirely filtered through Baynes' perceiving intelligence and his feelings. Because of trickery and ignorance in this first story, Tom Baynes loses Betsy; she dies of a broken heart through no fault of his. They had been perfect lovers since they were children. Tom and Betsy grow up in adjoining fisherman's cottages. The families are poor, but Betsy's father has a great attraction for plants and animals. When he receives an unexpected legacy, he rents a farm and buys animals. Tom fears that Betsy will no longer be interested in him, but she assures him that she has not changed. Tom courts Betsy at the farm and takes special delight in helping her milk. The lawyer's clerk, Taylor, who had brought the family news of their fortune, also courts Betsy, and Betsy's father, anxious for a son-in-law more suitable to his new station in life, encourages the clerk. One evening when Tom is milking, Betsy flirts mildly with the visiting clerk. Tom, in frustration and exasperation with the clerk's city manners, turns the cow's teat and squirts the clerk full in the face. The clerk vows revenge; he comes back to the farm some months later to announce to Betsy and her family that Jinny Magee is pregnant by Tom. Tom denies the charge, but Jinny asserts under oath that he is father of her child.

Tom's mother urges him to marry Jinny, but Tom goes into exile and becomes a sailor. He returns from his first two-year voyage to discover Betsy dead of a broken heart: Taylor had told her that Tom was drowned at sea and no one bothered to check his story. After a second trip, Tom happens into a dock area public house in Liverpool where he discovers Jinny Magee dying. She then admits that Taylor paid her to accuse Tom; Tom adopts Jinny's child and takes him back to his mother's house on the Isle of Man. Once home, he finds Taylor at Betsy's grave. Instead of killing Taylor, as he had threatened he would, Tom realizes that they both had loved Betsy Lee not wisely but too well.

In its original text, "Betsy Lee" is a tale of genuine moving passion. Interesting passion is thwarted passion. In a world where men and women couple easily, there would be no passion, just sex. "Betsy Lee" is a Manx *Cavalleria Rusticana,* but the passions are more bottled up than in Italy or Sicily, and Brown's Manx are provincials rather than rustics. "Betsy Lee" is opera-like in its sudden moments of lyricism, as when Baynes talks about the beauty of cows, or describes Betsy's body language when the two court in the presence of her parents, or tells how Parson Gale enjoys fishing.

The revisions that Macmillan asked for in 1881 cut the passion and the lyricism. In Brown's first version, Tom Baynes is so passionate that we can well believe he might have fathered Jinny Magee's child. Tom's mother thinks the child is his, and Betsy Lee's death would make more sense if Tom were the father. Nineteenth-century writers had to be careful about irregular unions; less than twenty years later Thomas Hardy arranged a fake marriage before Alex d'Urberville seduced Tess. Neither Brown's original text nor his revision for Macmillan tells us who fathered Jinny's child, but in the original version Tom is himself a man who might have. When Tom stumbles into the room in the public house in Liverpool, Jinny says to him,

> "Tom Baynes! Tom Baynes! is it you? is it you?
> Oh can it be? can it be? can it be true?"
> Well, I cudn speak, but just a nod—
> "Oh it's God that's sent you — it's God, it's God!"
> And she gasped and gasped — "Oh I wronged you, Thomas!
> I wronged you, I did, but he made me promise—
> And here I'm now, and I know I'll not live—

[She then shows Tom her child]

> "That's the child!"
> She says, and *my God!* the woman smiled!
> So I took him up, *and I says — quite low —*
> *"Is it Taylor's?" I says;* "Oh no! no! no!"
> *"All right!" I says; "and* his name?" "It's Simmy."

The italicized words are not published in the *Poems;* instead we read:

> "That's the child!"
> She says, and she smiled! the woman smiled!
> So I took him up, and — "His name?" "It's Simmy."

Since Jinny is dying in a very low house that caters to down-and-out sailors, the "My God" seems appropriate and right. Tom would want to know if the lawyer's clerk, Taylor, sired the child since he immediately adopts the child. When Tom discusses the matter with Parson Gale, he never states that he or anyone else is the father; Mrs. Gale and the servant snigger and grin, but Tom refuses to be concerned. Tom later rhapsodizes on the sleeping

Simmy, and his mates tease him for his affection. In one of the later
tales he calls Simmy his son. The original text is more satisfying.
Tom has spent all of his money on an after-voyage spree, and so he
must beg his way and beg food for the child as he makes his way
back to the Isle of Man and his mother who willingly takes the child
in. In a world where elementary relations between men and women
must be obscured, all hints may have meaning. Further, much of
TEB's story is communicated by indirection and suggestion;
reshufflings damage the whole fabric. Tom Baynes takes great
delight in rolling in the hay with Betsy; he is alert to generative
ideas, and he quickly assumes a father's role. If Tom is really the
father, Betsy's heartbreak is more explicable.

When the legacy first comes to the family, Tom fears to renew his
courtship. Betsy seems like a statue to him, and he can't speak to
her.

> And I tried, and I tried hard enough to speak,
> But I couldn' — then all of a sudden she turned,
> And the far-off look was gone, and she yearned
> To my heart, and she said: — "You doubted me."   (I, 103)

Tom has doubted, but he learns not to. If in a parallel situation,
Tom does give Betsy cause for doubt, then the story of "Betsy Lee"
is much more of a tragedy of separation.

The revision TEB made cuts out the original framework almost
entirely. In all the stories, Tom Baynes speaks to a listening
audience. Probably to Mr. Craik in London this repartee between
Tom and his hearers seemed unnecessary to the progress of the
story, idle fo'c's'le chatter, mere color. Brown's revision leaves in
only sufficient talk with his mates for us to keep in mind that we are
hearing the story aboard a ship. In TEB's first published text, Tom
Baynes must defend his right to tell his story and defend his right to
love. The love — since it is never fulfilled — seems absurd or
ridiculous to Tom's fellow sailors. By sheer force of words Tom
must persuade the sailors (and the reader) that his manly love is
valid and strong. In the following lines (cut from the received text)
Tom asserts his control over his laughing compeers; we can imagine
their bawdy suggestions; his drink with them certifies their agreement to listen respectfully:

Her father and mine used to hob-and-nob,
Being next-door neighbours — avast that Bob!
You didn laugh? you lubberly skunk!
It's div'lish nice for a fool in his bunk
To be lyin and laughin, and me goin on
And a tellin such things — now isn it, John?
Eh, Bill? He says he — *meant nothin by it?*
Well, I only want the chap to be quiet.
For there's wounds, my mates, that won't take healins,
And if a man's a man, he's got his feelins.
All right! I thank you, William my lad,
I will just taste it — it's not so bad.
(following *Poems* I, 98, line 58)

Craik in London — reading just for the story — would be bored by such play, but the play is essential to Brown's strategy. This play may be the "original motive" that Brown refers to in his letter to Macmillan asking that the cuts be restored. Brown, as in his lyric poems, writes about the joy and pain of slightly mad men. Tom Baynes, in his deep love for Betsy, is slightly mad to all his shipmates. His love for Betsy, beyond all reason, marks his "Keltic soul," and unless he can prove it to his shipmates in the same present with his readers (and not simply in the past of the narrative), then the story will not work. Tom knew joy and pain in the event; he knows joy and pain in the retelling. Thus we in the reading audience are more fully soothed by his humanity, by his very human love.

Although so much nineteenth-century writing is about feeling — Tennyson's *In Memoriam* or Dickens in *Bleak House* — later readers must sense that the century was genuinely frightened by the power of human emotions. Dickens, for example, suppressed and sublimated his actual passion for a young actress. Mrs. Gaskell never adjusted her admiration of George Eliot as a writer with her knowledge of George Eliot's irregular union. George Eliot's characters never could do what George Eliot did. Tom Baynes' story is about a consuming passion — such as George Eliot lived but never quite wrote about. Craik, the Victorian editor, would therefore ask that the passion be cut (recall that John Percival made his scholars keep their legs covered when playing soccer), that it be made tamer.

In the following lines, Tom Baynes explains how love creeps up on a man. He says that love comes

> Just like a clap of shoot or a squall,
> Or a snake or a viper, or some such dirt,
> Creep — creep — creepin under your shirt,
> And slidin and slippin right into your breast,
> And makin you as you can't get rest:
> And it works and it works till you feel your heart risin —
> God knows what it is if it isn pisin.   (*Poems* I, 9)

The published text stops there, but originally Brown had Baynes go on to specify the feelings in the legs. Craik might well have feared the elemental sexuality in the following lines:

> You've bathed in a dub that had seaweed in it,
> And just dropt your legs to rest for a minute,
> And let them go lazily dingle — dangle —
> And felt them caught by the twistin tangle —
> That's somethin like the kind of job;
> But ah, I loved Betsy, I did — now, Bob!

Brown's statement of passion beyond the control of the individual, this force in the "twistin tangle," frightens. In other lines removed Tom answers an attack from one of his listeners that Betsy Lee is of easy virtue, and Tom contrasts Betsy's virtue with the absence of virtue he has seen on Liverpool streets. Nineteenth-century London teemed with prostitutes but rarely could the literature of the time admit it. Dickens had to use all sorts of innuendo when he introduced a prostitute into *David Copperfield.* Dickens knew; he collected funds and established a home to reform wayward women, but he could not put one in his novel. So Brown must cut the mention to prostitutes on the streets of Liverpool. Keep naked sexuality hidden.

Brown had to cut not simply references to sex but other references to bodily functions. Originally Brown had used the body, like some twentieth-century writers, to speak beyond words. The following lines describe a stinking old man, but the stinking old man happens to own land and therefore he must be endured in the small farmhouse room:

> A lean, ould, hungry, mangy sinner!

> Hitched up all taut on the edge of his chair —
> And his guts stowed away with him — well, God knows where.
> And he'd sit and he'd talk! well, the way he'd talk!
> And he'd groan in his innards, and retch and hawk —
> And — "Scuse me!" he'd say, "it's my stemmick, marm!"
> And wasn it him that owned the farm?
> And of course ould Anthony made a fuss
> About him, but I didn care a cuss.

Brown's revisions remove the odor; Craik would say he was bored. In the revision Tommy Tite is simply described as a cunning man who would "groan in his innards." Brown's text has been fumigated.

Both versions of the story are comic, but the original text is more comic with its stinking old men and its lovers. In the original version Tom and Betsy are courting in an apple orchard; the original lost an effective rhyme which is both amusing and true:

> In the orchard we were, and the apple blossom
> Was shreddin down into Betsy's bosom,
> And I was pickin them out, d'ye see?

In the available edition, the lines read,

> In the orchard — and the apple blossoms there
> Was shreddin' down on Betsy's hair,
> And I was pickin' them off, d'ye see?   (I, 108)

In the nineteenth-century genteel society learned to speak about white and dark meat of a chicken to avoid references to chicken breast and legs. In a "drawing-room book" one would not think that bodies exist under the drapes. We may have such animal-like parts, but the higher view feared even to laugh at the pleasures of a young woman's bosom. Brown cut the "coarse" description of the young lovers in a winter-time cow stable:

> And *lastly,* as the Pazons is sayin, it's there
> You'll have your gel, if anywhere —
> All your own among the hay,
> Wrapped in your arms! and the things that she'll say,
> And the things that she'll do, you could hardly tell
> Before that she loved you half as well.

Such marvelous antics had to disappear, for what sophisticated Londoner wants to think what provincials might do in a hay mow!

In its original text, "Betsy Lee" is livelier, funnier, and a much more human poem. Selwyn Simpson, the first critic to write extensively about TEB, compared "Betsy Lee" to Tennyson's "Enoch Arden," to show that Brown's poem surpasses the laureate's.[10] Tennyson too wrote about provincial love that seems hardly possible to sophisticates. Tennyson, however, was slumming; he viewed always from the outside and his audience was asked to see his seaport lovers as if Enoch, Philip, and Annie Lee were some kind of savages who had acquired manners. Brown, however, tells Tom Baynes' story from inside Tom Baynes' world — the fo'c's'le, the farmhouses, and a Liverpool slum. Tennyson's "Enoch Arden" is — to its absolute ruin — middle class; Brown's fishermen, farmers, and sailors are men of a certain order in society who know, taste, and love. Tennyson is not funny except when we laugh at his quaint interjection of middle-class values. Brown triumphantly avoided Tennyson's errors, but his Macmillan editors were trying to put the genteel back into his manuscript. They cut Tom's speaking voice, the comedy, and the energy and very nearly ruined the poem; the text should be restored.

II   *The Passion of Christmas Rose*

On orders from his London publisher, Brown also cut "Christmas Rose." Christmas Rose is the name Parson Gale gives to a child, the only survivor from a December shipwreck on the southern coast of the island. A Negro sailor swims ashore holding the child by a sling in his mouth. Parson Gale adopts the child and raises her with his two sons, George and James. When the child is rescued from the beach (the sling has to be cut from the dead Negro's mouth), Parson Gale himself nurses her. Mrs. Gale is a cold, disapproving woman (like the Englishwoman on the Pincian at Rome) who has little love for her own child, but Parson Gale's love includes the dark-haired, foreign Christmas and Tom Baynes, now living with Parson Gale. The story thus moves to another stratum of Manx society, but impossible unions are still the subject. Again, the impossible unions are more evident and more moving in Brown's original text. Again the original text has more lambent lyricism; if all art, as Pater said, strives toward music, "Christmas Rose" is closer to music in the original text.

Tom Baynes skips quickly over the early years of childhood in this story and next tells about taking George, James, and Rose out with him in his fishing boat. When a storm comes up, Tom knows that they should return to shore, but Rose is marvelously stimulated by the storm and pleads for them to stay. The furious exertion that they must make to get the boat behind a protecting island is too much for James. He collapses. Tom orders Rose to nurse James while he and George continue to work the boat back to safe harbor. Safely at home, James confesses to Tom that he loves Rose and that he fears Rose loves his brother George more. Since Rose will not encourage James at all, the boy loses his will to live and dies. George next tries to woo Rose, but Rose insists that she can only love him as a brother. Tom also confesses that he loves Rose, but Tom confesses to George and not to Rose. If Rose loves anyone, she loves Parson Gale.

George, in despair, spends time in the public house. He enters a partnership fishing with Tom in order to earn money for his drinking. Once when they are out fishing, they see Rose on shore; they row in and find her fainting. George picks her up and, in the full version, he kisses her wildly. Tom Baynes is shocked but he does not stop George. When George goes to Oxford to become a preacher, he continues his spendthrift ways. Mrs. Gale asks Mrs. Lee (Betsy's mother: thus Tom knows this part of the story) to talk to Christmas Rose about the fact that she is causing George's ruin. Mrs. Gale has never loved any child and she cruelly rejects Rose once more. Further Mrs. Gale knows that Rose has more of the Parson's affection than she. George leaves Oxford, takes up with a hurdy-gurdy girl, and then emigrates to Australia. Rose, one late summer day, goes out on a headland during a storm. She is killed by a stroke of lightning and Tom finds her. She is buried beside the Negro:

> And to this day there's no man knows
> Who or what was the Christmas Rose.

As with "Betsy Lee," one out of seven lines in "Christmas Rose" is altered between the first and second edition. The changes follow the same patterns: cut the frame, cut the expletives, and tone down the references to bodily functions. Since "Christmas Rose" is much less the country idyl, the cuts are more damaging. When the child is first rescued from the ship, a nurse has to be found. The parson's comment is deleted in the later edition:

> For a nuss, and an aunt of mine bedad!
> Bless me the diddy that woman had!
>   [Diddy: dialect for breast with milk]
> Went up every day to give it the bress —[11]

The chief changes, however, are to reduce the attraction that Tom feels for the boys. The following lines are cut entirely:

> *Fond* was it I said I was? chit-chit!
> *Fond's* not the word, no nor a bit —
> I was mad after them two boys, I was —
> Mad — d'ye hear? why tben Doodoss! [a Manx expletive]
> Ware ye navar in love with a boy? *What way?*
> Well that's the thing I cannot say —
> *Like a brother or what?* no! no! no! no!
> *What do I mean?* Well wait then. Joe!
> Wait my lad! What I mean is willin
> To die for them two in a minute, a-spillin
> My last drop of blood, if so be it was wanted
> For the gud of them, and haunted lek, haunted
> With their look and their laugh — do ye follow the thing?
> Worshipin! Worshipin! worshipin!
> That's it — aye!

>   (Cockermouth text, pp. 11-12; *Poems* I, 142, middle)

At the end of the paragraph in the present text, the original text has these lines:

> And I've seen them bathin, and I don't care
> But I've felt that shamed and confused, d'ye hear?
> That I've looked (you may laugh, but what's the odds?)
> To see were they men or a sort of gods.

>   (Cockermouth text, p. 12)

The published text also omits twenty-four lines in which Tom Baynes explains how he could love both Betsy and Christmas Rose. Rose is his Queen of Heaven (he compares her to the pictures he has seen of madonnas in Rome), and Tom knows that he has no chance except to admire Rose from afar.

"Christmas Rose" belongs to that nineteenth-century tradition that connected wild, stormy nature with wild, stormy personality. In the twentieth century, we say that Rose represents the Dionysian energy that the nineteenth century suppressed. Mrs. Gale, who is always presented as a proper, class-conscious woman, fears Rose and denies her any love. Mrs. Gale is like the Englishwoman in Brown's lyric poem, "Roman Women"; in that poem, it will be remembered, he balances a cold, proud Englishwoman against the warmth and love of the Roman women. Rose (a kind of Aphrodite) is born out of the sea in a storm and returns to the elements in a storm. She is the Dionysian release that George, James, Tom, and even Parson Gale long for but can not reach.

In "Christmas Rose" TEB writes again about impossible unions. Although both sons love Christmas Rose, she herself loves Parson Gale. Mrs. Gale cannot love; she denies her humanity and cuts herself off from husband, children, and Christmas Rose. Not only is Mrs. Gale jealous, but she understands that her husband's love enriches his life as she cannot. In Brown's Manx world, the Manx can understand this love, but outsiders like the lawyer's clerk in "Betsy Lee" or Mrs. Gale in this story cannot understand basic human love. At first reading, Brown's ending, as in many of the lyrics, may seem an attempt to settle conflict by a simple catastrophe; sending off a character by a stroke of lightning is too convenient. He thus, we may think, avoids solution. In the world of Parson Gale's vicarage, the cool, objective Apollo cannot join the warm passionate feeling of Dionysus. Male and female can never meet. Christmas Rose returns to the elements because she too is elemental. The ending, in fact, supports the vision in all TEB's poems: pure love unites only with pure love and it is enough if we can know that purity in the art world.

"Christmas Rose" is more dramatic than "Betsy Lee." Its language is more vital; the sentiment evolves more obviously from the material. Brown beautifully suggests the excitement and movement of the Manxmen waiting to scavenge the wrecked ship. The public house scene where Tom and George spend summer evenings drinking beer has the sharp clarity that genre pictures demand; Millais or Burne-Jones might have painted it. In one of the most amusing scenes, Mrs. Gale and Mrs. Baynes banter hypocritically. The scene satirizes the drawing-room conventions that the provincials ape. The deaths that are so much a part of TEB's narrative stem naturally from the events; young James Gale does overexert himself in rowing to safety during the storm; Rose regularly seeks to front storms. Like "Betsy Lee," its text should be restored to that original passionate, lyrical form where names are named and passions are passions.

III   *The Sea Captains*

"Captain Tom and Captain Hugh"[12] (1873) is set in seaside dwellings and in the Irish Sea off the coast of the Isle of Man. This time Brown can concentrate on seascapes that remind his reader of Winslow Homer. The humor here is more muted and subordinated to the strange antagonism between the two brothers who are also captains. Brown uses his own name and the name of his brother Hugh; he may be sublimating his feelings for his brother. Captain Tom and Captain Hugh are, like Thomas Edward Brown and Hugh Stowell Brown, men set on different tracks and yet the tracks converge in destructive ways. Some inner daimon drives Captain Hugh. The story never quite names the daimon, but clearly the daimon is thwarted passion. The "Keltic souls" have passions too deep for tears, and yet the passions are made visible in this story. One regrets that Hugh Stowell Brown left no record of his response to the story; he probably thought it only some mad rantings that he would prefer not to think about. This story too is full of lyricism and passion that the London editors wanted cut.

The two sea captains, Tom and Hugh, have grown up together, learned navigation together, married sisters, and live in adjacent shore houses. The sister-wives have a brother, Ned Ballachrink, who is a kind of incubus in the story. In the original text, we learn that the brothers had their children at the same time. The families share, for a time, a garden behind the two houses.

The wives' brother, Ned Ballachrink, is passionately interested in the children. Since Ned is a drunkard, the sisters strive to keep him away from the children. When the owner for whom the captains sail decides to build a schooner, the whole community begins to speculate whether Tom or Hugh will be selected to captain the new ship. The reader knows that Tom will get the ship because Tom is presented as the calmer and steadier of the two, Hugh, for all his excellence, is moody, bitter-tongued, and ready to dispute. Ned Ballachrink, however, sees a chance to stir up trouble between the two men in hopes that their fight will allow him to get more chance to be with the children. In the quarrel which he starts, he backs the moody Hugh. After Tom is selected to be master of the schooner, Captain Hugh seizes every opportunity to race the schooner. The story ends with Hugh senselessly keeping his sails on when a storm strikes the two ships in the Irish Sea. His son is rescued but Captain Hugh refuses the rope thrown to him and works out of the noose that Captain Tom throws around him. He drowns. His son Hughie then marries Captain Tom's daughter.

The children in the family have been raised as brother and sister, but when they come of an age, they fall in love. The mothers encourage the union and fear the response of the fathers when they hear. Captain Tom is very pleased about the union. Captain Hugh makes no particular response to the news; he is phlegmatic and refuses to rise to the bait when the women in the community try to tease him.

Ned, who always likes to tell other people how to conduct their business, tries to tell Captain Hugh to reef his sail in the storm, but Hugh strikes him. Ned falls on a hatch and into the sea. At his death, Ned's fortune goes to Annie, Captain Tom's daughter. The hedge that Ned Ballachrink had planted between the two gardens is torn down.

The story has much in common with the other stories in Brown's Manx epic. Again, since young Hughie and Annie are raised together, the central love affair is incestuous. Tom is more than a little in love with Annie, but now Tom Baynes is clearly too old to do anything but admire her youthful bloom. Ned Ballachrink's excess and impossible love for the children follows a familiar pattern in the stories. Young Hughie loves his father in excess, but the father ignores his son. Even though young Hughie becomes a superb sailor, his father only grudgingly acknowledges him. Blighting love is again Brown's subject. Again the Manx fail to comprehend the new technology from England. Tom Baynes is most contemptuous of the schooner, a new-fangled ship style that ought to be avoided. Baynes, like all Manx characters in these stories, clings to old ways.

In cutting his text thirteen percent, Brown cut so that the love affair between the young Hughie and Annie becomes conventional. Early in the poem he dropped twenty lines on the alteration when love first strikes consciousness. He also cut the references to the listening sailors in the fo'c's'le who object to another love story.

The major reduction, however, comes near the end when Brown excised one hundred lines on the relations between young Annie and her uncle, the father of her lover. Before the final race between Tom and Hugh, Hugh sends for Annie and talks to her alone for more than half an hour. The women listen at the door, but they can't hear any conversation. When Annie comes out from the interview, she is described as being in a kind of ecstasy:

and the lep [lip]
The tight, and the nails dug into the hands,
And the fingers at her just like strands
Clinched, and the head thrown back like a hoss's.
Lek you'll see these picthurs of people on crosses,
With their body all stretched like steel, like wire,
With their noses all spreadin' lek with fire,
Lek lifted up, lek crucified —
The love, the misery, the pride —
My gough! — They're knowin' what you're not knowin',
They're seein' him upon the throne.   (p. 31, Douglas text)

Tom Baynes says that she is "changed" after the experience, and she sits "like seein' things unseen." When young Hughie says that he thinks his father "wrong in the head," she denies it. In the section of the story after the death of Hugh, Brown cut sixty more lines which tell about Annie's fierce reaction to news of Captain Hugh's death. She has dreams and utters wild questions. Doctor Bell is called in; he advises patience, that time will heal her, and it does. But the Annie who survives is a strengthened woman: "her sorrow ... Went down for ever with Captain Hugh" (p. 37, Douglas text). And so the marriage is more stable since Annie is a wiser woman.

Restoring the cuts would not clarify the daimon that drove Hugh, but would give the poem a richer and more mystifying sense of human engagement. The reader has no idea what happened between Hugh and Annie in the room, nor does he have any idea why Hugh must rival Tom at every opportunity. It is not sufficient to say he was disappointed that Captain Tom commands the schooner, for that rivalry was manufactured by Ned Ballachrink. The inexplicable character of the rivalry is enhanced in the full version of the story. Flaubert would have loved the purity with which Brown presents his material, without a trace of authorial comment. Tom Baynes comments but, as always, we know the origin of his judgments.

The perversion of love in Mrs. Gale has moved from a minor position in her story to become the major interest in "Captain Tom and Captain Hugh." The force against love is as strong here as the force toward love in "Christmas Rose." The elements also destroy Hugh, but his destruction inverts the ending of "Christmas Rose." To reduce Brown's story to dull, psychiatric terms, Hugh has reached the crisis of middle age; he cannot accept his aging nor his loss of vital powers. Thus he imagines the impossible union with his son's intended. Some impossible unions are impossible. Hugh's death at sea is the suicide of a man unable to resolve his emotions and the facts of his life. Again Brown's story pushes into forbidden territories of the human spirit; a familiar defense is the so-called boredom claimed by Mr. Craik in London. No doubt Craik was right; the reading public would have feared to enter the strange province of Brown's story. Full expression almost requires music. Benjamin Britten, after he wrote *Peter Grimes,* might have made an opera of this story.

IV *A Northern Farm*

Brown ran smack into another taboo when he wrote "Tommy Big-Eyes" (1879–80). He objected in his original letter on the cutting process that Tom Baynes had been cut in his texts. In the other stories, Tom Baynes likes to make parallels to Biblical stories, but the parallels do not materially change the stories although they add to the richness of the texture. In "Tommy Big-Eyes" a religious question stands in the middle of the story, for the villain is a Bible-quoting Methodist minister. Brown blamed the cuts also on "Methodism and Macmillanism."[13] Macmillan had a long history of publishing for the Bible trade. Even as late as 1954, the company worried about the propriety of Keltic words used in a Sean O'Casey play.[14] Many readers on the Isle of Man were Methodists or sympathizing Low Church, and the Methodist audience in England was sizeable enough so that losing it would limit the profit from the book. The large-scale publishing ventures in the nineteenth century had to be just as alert to ripples in the market place as twentieth-century television companies. "Tommy Big-Eyes" had to be adjusted for the Methodists, and the Methodist villain had to be toned down to more conventional expectations of behavior. Brown's irony and Brown's satire (two dangerous forces in the century) had to be circumscribed.

The story again is simplicity itself, and the narrative method is to expand details of the action into lyric expressions or full rendering of dramatic scenes. In the first lines Tom Baynes announces the interest of the story:

> I never knew a man in my life
> That had such a darling little wife

As a chap they were callin Tommy Gellin;
So how he got her is worth the tellin.
                        (*Poems* I, 222, punctuation
                                 of Douglas text)

We learn about Tommy as a schoolboy when he first meets Ellen (or Nelly) Quine. When they leave school, Tommy becomes a servant at Renshent, a farm operated by Mr. and Mrs. Cain, and Nelly becomes a servant at the neighboring Ballaglass where the Moore family lives. Tommy is a great favorite at his farm because he plays the violin so well; Mrs. Cain is especially pleased by the gaiety he brings to the house. Her husband, a Methodist, decides that Tommy should learn to play the viol-bass for the chapel.

Tommy is too shy to court Nelly Quine, but he sneaks to the neighboring farm and watches the other young couples courting. Thus he accidentally discovers that young Captain Moore is courting Nelly. When he tells Mrs. Cain what he has discovered, she tells him she loved the boy's father; because the marriage was prevented, she entered a loveless marriage with Cain. Again TEB roots his story in an impossible union. Mrs. Cain tries to warn Nelly, but Nelly and the young man escape from the island. They sail out in a storm and the boat is forced back to the shore. Tom Baynes swims out to rescue Nelly, but young Captain Moore dies in the wreck.

When Nelly becomes a servant at Renshent, the Cain farmhouse, Old Cain begins to pay particular attention to her. Since Nelly is now fatherless, she takes his concern to be that of a father. Tommy, in the meantime, has left the farm. When he finds Nelly's mother in Douglas, a widow without any place to live and no support, he offers her his room. Cain's Methodist churchmen find Cain's attachment for Nelly too scandalous. When Cain finally makes a protest of love to Nelly, she runs to Mrs. Cain for protection. Mrs. Cain, recognizing her own guilt in not loving Cain, commits suicide. Cain, immediately after the funeral, asks Nelly to be his wife, but Nelly threatens to put a knife in his back. When Cain returns with the same plea, Nelly again threatens him, but this time Cain has two policemen as witness. Nelly is charged with the murder of Mrs. Cain. Tommy, who has succeeded very well in Douglas, hires a lawyer who threatens Cain with arrest as a co-conspirator unless Cain gives up the suicide note. Cain flees to America and Nelly is set free. Renshent farm goes to an English heir, but Tommy rents it and he lives there with Nelly, his wife.

Quite clearly the story furthers a plan to encompass all Manx life. The story takes place on the northern part of the island (all the others had been placed near Castletown in the south). The northern third of the Isle of Man is a flat, open plain, where the soil tends to be boggy unless it is drained. Brown's mentor, Joseph Christian Moore, lived at Kirk Andreas, almost in the center of the area. Neighboring farms, Ballacaine (*balla* is Manx for *farm* and it is the Manx custom to add the family name) and Ballamoar Castle, might well be the models for Renshent and Ballaglass.

If the story were all-important, then Craik, the Macmillan editor, was right in cutting the length of it. Since the story is the minor consideration, the cuts deprive readers of Brown's lyric flight. The following section refers to a hen that Tommy Big-Eyes brought to school to give to Nelly. The hen got out of its basket and disrupted the school. Tom Baynes and his friend decide to pay a visit to Nelly since she did not return to school after the incident:

> There was Nelly at the door,
> Sittin on the step, and rockin'
> The baby in her arms, that was cryin' shockin'.
> So I leaned on the hedge there, *just like this,*
> And "My compliments, Miss Quine," I says;
> "You'll 'scuse our callin' without any warnin':
> And how is Tommy's hen this mornin'?"
> Oh she made a grab, and a stone at her foot
> As big as a turmit — didn't we cut?
> But shoutin' all the way down the glen —
> "Tommy's hen! Tommy's Hen!"
> And finished off with three good cheers,
> And I don't think I saw her again for years.

> (p. 13, Douglas text. Emphasis added.)

The gesture, "just like this," both clarifies the original scene and reminds us that Tom Baynes engages in remembrance of things past. Tom *tells* his hearers what fiends children are in their teens, but the story of his visit makes the judgment sharp. Tom condemns the other children in school for teasing Tommy Big-Eyes for his shyness and for the fancy clothes his mother sends him to school in, but this scene shows Tom's own cruelty at the same time it renders the quality of childhood. Brown makes a terrifying and exact psychological observation about childhood designed, almost, to arouse Craik's boredom defense.

In the revision, as always, the expletives disappear or become so
mild as to be utterly invisible. The shock value of a good cuss word
shows Brown working a method that resembles the method of
Robert Burns in "Holy Willie's Prayer," where the supposed pious
speech of a man condemns him as an absolute hypocrite. The
method is dangerous since readers may take the sense and let the
meaning go.

Cain, the Methodist, has money to put out at interest. In fact, he
holds a mortgage on the chapel itself, and he uses his economic
power to try to persuade the chapel-attenders to act in ways pleasing to him. The following words, from the original text, employ
Brown's familiar device of italicizing material from imagined con-
versations:

> *But still he counted all but loss* —
> "A humble servant of the cross,"
> He said — and *the people liked him,* he said,
> *And who was he to deny the bread*
> *Of life to hungry sinners? No!*
> He said *he didn' want to go*
> *And leave the little flock that loved him* —
> And d____ him! if they'd took and shoved him
> Over the brews —
>
> (p. 19, Douglas text. Lines removed at I, 239)

The blank, unspelled word of Tom's interjection is clear enough
and valuable enough to keep. By this stage in the story we perfectly
agree that Cain should be damned and thrown over a cliff (the
brews). Later when Tommy Big-Eyes so befuddles the congregation
by improvising on the hymn tune, Cain says

> "Take the viol from him!
> Lick him! kick him! smash him! d____ him!"
> *Did he? In the chapel too!* I'll engage
> He did: and wasn he black with rage.
>
> (Douglas text, pp. 26–27; *Poems,* I, 247).

Saying the word *damn* interests Tom's sailor audience, especially
since Cain says it in the chapel. The word is also funny at that place
in the story. It is also funny when, in the original text, a preacher in
Douglas once told Cain that he looked like a man who was first see-

ing Canaan. Cain's promised land is usually the sight of money or, as the reference is repeated, when he looks at Nelly Quine.

Some of the cuts amuse us looking back from the perspective of one hundred years. Tommy Big-Eyes finds Nelly Quine in a summer house with young Captain Moore. In the published version, the lines read,

> And — aw, poor Tommy! lips to lips,
> Yes, yes! aw Tommy my son,
> You're beat! you're beat! the game is won!   (I, 257)

In the original Douglas text, the lines read,

> And — aw, poor Tommy! lips to lips,
> Breast to breast, aw Tommy my son,
> You're beat! you're beat! the game is won!   (p. 36, Douglas)

The Douglas text here is superior.

But chiefly the story is changed. In the original version, Mrs. Cain married Cain in expectation that he would help her prepare for the life to come. Since she could not marry Captain Moore, she had no expectation for this life. Cain, on his part, wanted her farm. He also decided that he wanted the charming young woman that he had married. She refused his love. In the original version Brown makes quite explicit the fact that the marriage was never consummated. Thus Mrs. Cain's interest in Tommy's music, and Cain's own passionate attraction to Nelly Quine follow as a much more natural consequence. Of the four stories in *Fo'c's'le Yarns: First Series,* "Tommy Big-Eyes" most competently motivates the action. The narrative would be more complete if the poem had been allowed to stand as Brown wrote it.

The Macmillan editors could not entirely destroy the poems, but they have been changed, muffled, and dimmed. The fact of the changes being made, however, indicates another quality about the audience. George L. Craik, from all evidence, was a literate, intelligent man, but he completely misjudged the nature of Brown's work. He read the stories as if they were narratives, but the *story* is the least interesting part of the writing. As with Dickens and other Victorians, Brown used the story as a vehicle to convey character, incident, and natural description. If the audience demanded story, then the writers were perfectly willing to give the audience what it wanted. Brown has the mystery and the magic that his audience expected; with that demand satisfied, he turned Tom Baynes loose on the pleasure of describing how a fugue works or the appearance of Tommy Gellin's big eyes, of recounting the play of rhetoric when Cain tells Tommy that his soul will be saved if he plays a viol-bass at chapel.

Twentieth-century readers should avoid the error of wanting just the story. A reader might wish to have the narratives in prose to compare them to short stories of American local color writers. John Addington Symonds thought that the stories might be printed like Brett Harte's,[15] and evidently Brown's other friends urged him to use more available and more popular forms. In his last years on the Isle of Man, Brown published a short fiction in a Manx newspaper.[16] The story has all the familiar ingredients — setting, love, and mystery — but without verse, it is utterly flat.

We could expect Brown to defy the traditions of his time to write his Manx epic. His friends Hall Caine and John Quine wrote successful novels. One of Hall Caine's novels was the first book to sell over one million copies. Brown's genius was lyrical, not novelistic. Portions of his stories are pulled out of contexts for recitation each May at the Manx Festival in Douglas. The audience, of course, knows the whole context, and the selections move deeply by the sheer power of their lyricism. Had the phonograph been invented in time, Brown might have had a career somewhat like that of Dylan Thomas. When Tom Baynes describes children on the beach, Tommy Gellin playing his viol-bass, the sight of Christmas Rose, or how the Gale boys looked naked, then the poems lighten up with incandescence. A speaking Manx voice transforms the words on the page into music.

TEB wrote these poems in isolation at Clifton; the musical sound of the Manx speech soothed and eased him from his drudgery as a master. He says also in his Oxford essay that want of society drives a man inward; Brown's want of society at Clifton drove him inward to these Manx narratives. Also, in writing about impossible union after impossible union, Brown wrote on a subject that dull prose can only imperfectly encompass. One thinks of Hardy but Hardy's novels came after Brown. Brown, surprisingly, did not like *Tess of the D'Urbervilles* when it was first published. TEB thought the Stonehenge scene too stagey, written simply to extend the novel for serial publication; he objected to the marriage of Angel Clare and Liza-Lu as have many other readers. Chiefly Brown suspected that Hardy did not know Tess.[17] Especially in stories like "Tommy Big-Eyes" and "Captain Tom and Captain Hugh," Brown did know his characters so that he could sing their own song. He could not always put into prose what he knew about them (as with Captain Hugh's mad infatuation for his niece), but verse does allow room for violent, inexplicable passion. Brown's subjects required verse, not prose, just as Hardy's did, and he too turned to verse. Brown sought a *dolce far niente* beyond prose.

It also seems clear that a Manx epic required a language capable of more sinuous, musical meanings to communicate the "Keltic souls" of his subjects. Inside the vision of Tom Baynes, TEB had much more room to move through Manx life from the perspective of a man whose view is pure and uncontaminated by false sophistication or false learning. Tom renders simple sensualities because he knows them. His vision has the "strength and healthy balance of mental parts" which Tillyard defines as essential to the writing of epic.[18] Brown thus could best pursue his strategy to "unlock the treasures of the Island heart"; he would fix "upon the page" the old heritage, manners, speech, polity, and humor which Tom Baynes finds and makes. Tom Baynes sings the song of Manx life in the 1840s and 1850s. No steam locomotive dirties the air; the ships all move by sail. The only books known are *Robinson Crusoe, Pilgrim's Progress,* and the Bible. The occupations are farmer, fisher, sailor, parson; all his people, as Thoreau said, live deliberately. The Moore family in "Tommy Big-Eyes" marks the highest ascent in the social order that Tom can reach. Even life in that house is reported through the eyes of Manx servants. These simple, direct, and true men and women can best speak that old heritage. Thus Brown in the first four stories written early in the 1870s made a healthy start on his Manx epic, and he gambled all his talent on rendering one single vision. What he attempted is both exciting and awe-inspiring.

CHAPTER 8

Tom Baynes as Monologuist:
Fo'c's'le Yarns: Second Series

For it isn' every fool that's fit
To make a rael good lie, that'll sit
On her keel, and answer her helm.

"The Doctor," *Poems,* II, 2.

F OR centuries European writers shared the values and meanings of their audience; the writer translated the brass world of value and meaning into the golden world of his art. In the nineteenth century no writer could assume that his audience shared his truth. Wordsworth, beginning *The Prelude,* tells about his conviction that he should write, but that he found himself unable to judge the truth of possible subjects. He started to write an epic poem for his age, but ended by writing the story of his own growth toward knowledge and understanding. So much early nineteenth-century writing is personal, interior. With no way to know objective truth, the writers gave their readers subjective truth.[1] The art form of the century is a form for discovery of individual truth.

In the 1830s and 1840s both Tennyson and Browning discovered the dramatic monologue as an alternative to the confessional mode that dominated early nineteenth-century art. Instead of revealing their own agonies and secrets, they created men speaking at climactic moments in their lives. The characters themselves — always imperfect men whom we alternately pity and condemn — give us the facts by which we can judge them. The century was full of speculation about point of view, a critical intelligence, reversals from the familiar, and the truth of art. The word *sincerity* acquired for a moment, and then lost, its power, but even without the word itself the quality remained that signified the writer's ability to convince his reader that his perspective had validity.[2] Dickens, Jane Austen, Carlyle persuade us that their view has unquestionable certainty, sureness, completeness. The minute that the reader dares to question the point of view, the work of art falters and loses its charm.

Because Thomas Edward Brown uses an obvious *persona* in Tom Baynes and a language that is, on the surface, rough and rugged, critics have wanted to place Brown with Robert Browning. Browning's angularity resembles the hard angles in Brown. Both too make music out of ordinary speech rhythms, and both use the speaking voice of a created character to say what neither could have said in his own voice. The poet can experiment in those voices with strange values, new ideas, bold perspectives without ever damaging his own security. T. E. Brown also has an advantage in Tom Baynes, who can think and act and do what the Rev. T. E. Brown, late Fellow of Oriel and Master at Clifton College, could not think, act, or do. Tom Baynes is useful to Brown just as Browning's many characters were useful to him; these *personae* view a world in chaos where the only values are ways of seeing. No one can tell us which of the thirteen ways to look at a blackbird is the "right" way; therefore, let us see the blackbird as Tom Baynes, as the Duke of Ferrara, or as the many voices that speak in Browning's *The Ring and the Book*.

TEB differs, however, so fundamentally from Browning that the comparison confuses more than it clarifies. Browning has nothing comparable to TEB's Manx nationalism. Browning invents characters to discover new ways to meet the demands of a changing, fluid world. Browning's priests, noblemen and women, his artists are at the forward edge of society where values and meanings change bewilderingly. Thus Browning's "Fra Lippo Lippi" seeks to articulate a new role for art in society. TEB's Tom Baynes, at the very opposite, speaks to recover a vanishing past. Browning's characters speak to find out; TEB's Tom Baynes *knows*. Browning's men and women are outsiders; TEB's Tom lives inside a special world. Browning's reprobates, murderers, thieves are at the opposite extreme from TEB's innocents with whom we sympathize entirely. Although Tom Baynes is very provincial (he thinks an English Midlands accent is French), he is never morally or psychologically outside the pale. He is, rather, an ordinary man discovering in the customs and myths of his people an extraordinary human quality: love. As a character, Tom Baynes expands but does not grow. We trust his vision into the heart of things. Although the comparison to Browning tempts TEB's readers, the comparison does not help us to understand the special character of TEB's writing.

Tom Baynes is a bachelor sailor interested in love. He is a Ulysses in exile, but his homeland is the Isle of Man, a nation nearly "Lost in the empire's mass."[3] He travels with a young sailor named Simmy, but between voyages he goes back to the island so that he may hold "as in a glass" that which is dear and meaningful in the old Manx life. For the sake of this exploration, Tom Baynes is the anti-mask of his creator. Baynes is everything TEB was not, but Baynes is everything that TEB might have imagined himself to be, a pure Kelt.

Brown did say he shared judgments with Baynes. Writing to a Clifton College friend, J. R. Mozley, in 1882 (just after the first series of *Fo'c's'le Yarns* was published), Brown said,

> You are quite right about these stories. Keltic, that is it; the Kelt emerging if you will, but the Kelt, if I may say so, a good deal hardened and corrupted by the Saxon. That is Tom Baynes; that is myself, in fact. I never stopped for a moment to think what Tom Baynes should be like; he simply is I, just such a crabbed text, blurred with scholia " in the margent," as is your humble servant. So when I am alone, I think and speak to myself always as he does.[4]

Notice, however, that Brown says that he speaks like Tom Baynes when he is alone. Brown thus refers again to that split between the inner life and the outer Kapelistic life that he lived. I have no doubt that Tom Baynes was Tom Brown in one aspect of his character. Tom Baynes is the free spirit that T. E. Brown desired to be but never succeeded in becoming. He is the mythic Keltic soul who almost unconsciously articulates the myths of his Keltic soul. He is the perfect front for TEB because he differs so much from the actual TEB.

I   *"The Doctor"*

The three tales in Brown's continuing Manx epic to be discussed here are "The Doctor," "Kitty of Sherragh Vane," and "The Schoolmasters." "The Doctor" was completed in the spring of 1876 before its publication that winter on the Isle of Man. The other two stories were not published before Brown brought them all together in 1887 in *"The Doctor" and Other Poems.*

"The Doctor" had acquired almost an underground reputation as a result of James Maurice Wilson, who read it in Italy. Brown, writing in 1886, said that Wilson read the poem in 1885 to

a set of people at the Malaga Hotel. Among these were Professor Max Müller and Mr. [William] Story, the [American] sculptor. Mrs. Story wrote to me for a copy, and Professor Max Müller, going on to Venice, met there the Crown Princess of Germany [Victoria's daughter], and read "The Doctor" to her. She asked for a copy, and I sent her one. Lastly Professor Müller mentions "The Doctor," in terms of extravagant eulogy, in the *Pall Mall* (some nonsense about "best books," the sort of fussy rubbish the *Pall Mall* occasionally goes in for).[5]

In such a heady set, TEB might have felt that his Tom Baynes was at last setting forth on the stormy seas of literature. Alas, it was not to be.

"The Doctor," the longest of the narratives, is the most ambitious in its range to London, and it connects love and duty. In the sequence of stories, Tom Baynes is less and less a participant. He does figure in parts of this story, but other sections are far beyond his life and his possible experience. The doctor, an Englishman named Bell, comes to the Isle of Man to recover from a disastrous love affair. He had fallen in love with Harriet, the daughter of his patron, Sir John. At a great party in Sir John's house, Dr. Bell and Harriet are discovered in the conservatory kissing. Bell is ordered out of the house. Harriet is sent to the Continent, and Bell searches fruitlessly for her. When he becomes ill, a physician friend urges him to retire to the Isle of Man to rest. Bell takes rooms at a Manx farmhouse where Mrs. Kelly, the owner's wife, judges him to be another drunken Englishman come for the cheap whiskey. Bell does not reveal himself as a physician.

During a great cholera epidemic (such an epidemic occurred in 1832), Bell ministers to the frantic community. When the epidemic has run its course, the community asks Bell to return to practice. The men build him a house and a boat to induce him to stay. Bell falls victim to the disease and retires to the loft of Mr. Kelly's barn. Although he had instructed the Kelly family to stay away, the daughter climbs up into the loft early in the morning. To send her back to her family would break the quarantine; Mr. Kelly demands to know if Bell's intentions are honorable. In despair, Bell marries the girl and becomes physician for the Lhen, Brown's imagined Manx village.

Bell and his Manx wife have two children, Mary and Will, and later a third child, Katty. For a period of time, Tom Baynes enters the story as Katty's companion. She accompanies Tom when he courts Betsy Lee. The doctor's wife cannot play her elevated role in life as a physician's wife. She had been "very lonely— / Sundherd from her own people, you see, / And makin' no friends with the quality" (II, 67). Tom Baynes describes her as a "Doeless woman."

Two weeks after the birth of Katty, a letter arrives from Harriet. Sir John has died and Harriet is still unmarried. Since Dr. Bell is out on a call, Mrs. Bell opens the letter. In a jealous rage, she refuses to nurse Katty or care for her other children. Since Bell is extremely busy, he cannot supervise his children. Except for Katty, they are wild and irresponsible. Once they explode a gun down Mrs. Baynes' chimney; they run off and spend a week living with gypsies; they steal money and jeer at their mother. Dr. Bell pleads with Tom Baynes to help make his children behave better. Tom seems to have some success with the daughter Mary, but only because she is under the influence of some drug. Both Will and Mary leave; the mother dies after the two eldest children disappear. Dr. Bell is more often drunk.

Under Tom's influence, Katty grows up as a responsible Victorian child. One evening a yacht puts into harbor; some of the crew go ashore in search of a physician. Dr. Bell is summoned and comes to the bedside of Harriet, who dies in his arms. With her are her husband and only son. Before the story ends, Katty and the son meet.

One understands why Queen Victoria's daughter, the Crown Princess of Germany, enjoyed the poem. It is a domestic tragedy with a seemingly strong man defeated by a foolish, ignorant woman. Had Dr. Bell remained true, he could have married Harriet, the woman whom he deserved. Unfortunately he was tricked into marriage and must suffer the hardship of a bad marriage. Tom tells the story to explain why the islanders accept a drunken doctor and why Dr. Bell is so devoted to his practice. The triumph of duty seems a topic certain to interest Queen Victoria's household.

Again the story gives Tom Baynes opportunity to create character, depict scenes, and comment on the old Manx life. "The Doctor," as a story, has exactly the function of story for nineteenth-century opera; the libretto has to exist so that the lyric moments can occur. As one hears stories about opera-audiences who went to the theater only to hear two or three arias, so a reader of "The Doctor'' waits for the aria-like moments when Tom Baynes describes the cholera epidemic (he admits that he could not have been present), Rutchie Fell (the Methodist boatbuilder) discovering the design for Dr. Bell's boat, or the comic description of Sir John's London party when Dr. Bell and Harriet are discovered kissing in the conservatory. Tom Baynes contrasts (his best technique) falling in love in the country with falling in love in town. We even hear about Tom Baynes' being jailed for drunkenness in Liverpool. The description of the villagers carting Mary Bell back to Douglas and putting her on the boat has the vitality of a good genre picture. The main story starts with the picture of the drunken physician and works back to those scenes that yield present fact and present judgment. Tom Baynes' method resembles the epic poet's beginning *in medias res,* but it differs because Tom Baynes cares so little about the story and so much about the emotions, the scenes, and the quality of life.

As in the other stories, Tom Baynes tells of thwarted and misdirected love. The relationship between Will and Mary Bell, like that between the children in ''Betsy Lee,'' ''Christmas Rose,'' or ''Captain Tom and Captain Hugh,'' is dangerously close. Will, who lasts only a term at the local school, spends time with the army officers in Douglas. He arranges for Mary to leave the island with one of his captain friends. Tom Baynes is sure of the cause of Mary's ruin:

> So that was Misther Willy Bell
> That sould [sold] his sisther. Still! — keep still!
> Sould her! Didn' I see the notes?
> And didn' I tell him *he had his wages,*
> *And he'd burn for it through all the ages*
> *Of hell,* I said, . . .   (II, 96–97)

When Mary returns to the village, she too is rejected as being unfit to live in the community. Parson Gale tries to reason with the men who cart her, but she is carried off, without even seeing her father, and put on the boat to England.

The harsh judgment against Willy Bell is uncharacteristic of Tom Baynes. It comes late enough in the story so that the reader makes the same judgment himself. Actually Tom Baynes is extremely tolerant. As he says,

> There isn't one of us hasn't a list

> To port or starboard, either way —
> "Some likes coffee, some likes tea!"   (II, 5)

He even tolerates Mrs. Bell:

> But as for her, she didn't bother
> Much about him, bein able to smother
> Her soul complete, or maybe for spite —
> I don't know, and it's hardly right
> To condemn the woman.   (II, 74)

When Mary Bell is ridden out of town, Tom follows the cart and ex-
cuses the poor woman: "for, for all the sinner / She was, the door
shouldn' be shut agin her" (II, 97). This quality of toleration has a
function in the series of stories. Because he is so tolerant and
accepting, Brown has little trouble persuading us of Baynes' knowledge of his stories. We learn several times in "The Doctor" about
his acquaintance with James, a servant in the London household.
James has not only told Baynes what happened in London, but also
this same James rows ashore at the end of the story to bring the
doctor for the dying Harriet. Tom takes the doctor out to the yacht,
but the little conjunction and our knowledge of Baynes' openness,
interest, and tolerance enables Brown to move his story with great
freedom. Because Baynes is tolerant and because evidently every
man he meets becomes a friend, "The Doctor" succeeds as a story
— even though so much of its action takes place beyond Tom
Baynes' ken.

Tom Baynes has another quality as a storyteller which aids his
art: he digresses. Details, however, from digressions suddenly
become relevant. In a section in which he has apparently gone far
away from his story to tell about Ruchie Fell's inspiration for
designing the Doctor's boat, Baynes not only gets carried away into
the subject of design but he knows that he threatens to run awry:

> but the trim's in the float —
> In the very make of her! That's the trimmin'!
> And, by gough, it's the same with men and women;
> For, look here! if a man — But, bless my soul!
> What's the odds! I'm runnin' foul
> Altogether, and no time to lose;
> But "Forge ahead!" says Billy Baroose.   (II, 63)

Since this whole discussion of designing a boat and the question of how it should be trimmed precedes Doctor Bell's marriage and follows his resumption of his career as a physician, the apparent digression turns out to be necessary to qualify and define the tone of Bell's life. Marriage and boatbuilding require thought. The seeming digressions serve, along with Baynes' tolerance and openness to friendship, to sustain the reader until the lyric moments occur.[6]

Baynes is visual in his reports. Late nineteenth-century art often astounds the reader by seeing with the eye of a movie camera. *Fo'c's'le Yarns* are not suitable for movie treatment, but they can be easily read by an imagination trained by motion pictures. Notice how the following lines create a running sequence of scenes that, quickly shifting, convey the meanness of Bell's children as they try to get revenge on Tom Baynes:

> They got a gun
> Betwixt them, and what do you think they done?
> Climbed up our roof — aw, she could do it nimbly —
> And took and fired it down the chimbly.
> And the soot comin' down in sheets; and the broth
> All spoilt; and mother fit to froth
> At the mouth with rage, and took a hatchet.
> "By Gough," says I, "it's now you'll catch it."
> But charges [re-loaded] so quick as they were able,
> And let drive again behind the gable.
> "Come here," says mother, "and I'll give you your lickin's!
> Come here," says she, "ye divil's chickens!"
> "Good even'! Mrs. Baynes," says they,
> And laughs, and laughs, and cuts away.   (II, 76–77)

It is as though Baynes' eyes were a camera seeing first the scene outside the cottage, then the interior, and then the exterior. He seems to be the living, concrete voice of the experience that he recounts.

"The Doctor" may be the best single poem in the sequence (Brown himself preferred "Tommy Big-Eyes"). The poem has virtuoso control of story and scene, and it has marvelous variety in its boat-building, epidemic, and tavern scenes. It is distinctive for having an Englishman as its hero, for its larger time span (nearly thirty years), and for its rich subject of human duty in adversity.

II *Mountain Farm*

When Brown finally published "The Doctor" in 1887, he added

two other narratives to fill out the book. Neither had been published before but they were probably written in the 1880s. In "Kitty
of the Sherragh Vane" Brown changed from his octosyllabic line of
the first five stories and used a line of varying length, often with
just two accents. The lines move quickly, but Tom Baynes is still
just as slow about the story. Again a love story is complicated
because of the closeness between brother and sister.

The story differs, however, in its setting and in its major figure.
This time we are in the northern mountains. The main action concerns Kitty Tear and her love, but the story is interesting for its picture of the mountain farmer, Nicholas Tear, her father. Tom
Baynes is an older man than in the previous five stories; he says he
could be Kitty's father (II, 115). He first meets the six-year-old
Kitty when he is lost in the mountains. He finds the child alone in
the house. She is not frightened by him nor by the wild, foggy
weather.

When he sees her grown up, she still has the same independent
spirit that he noticed in her as a child. At that time he is mate with
Saul Tear, her brother, aboard the *Mermaid,* and, home from a sea
voyage, Tom pays a visit at the mountain farm, Sherragh Vane. The
men in the fo'c's'le think that Tom might have fallen a little in love
with Kitty, but Tom explains that Saul was too jealous of her. Tom
visits the farm during the harvest season which is an excellent time
for courting. Kitty disappears on the open moor, and her brother
Saul watches her suspiciously: "he'd ha' twisted the neck / Of a
chap that dared to look at the gel" (II, 117). They have no clue to
explain her disappearance from the farm, and she returns to do her
work, but the brother keeps alert to discover her secret. He takes
Tom out with him ostensibly to hunt, but actually to follow a track
that he noticed his sister take. They find a sick man, wrapped in
quilts and blankets from Kitty's own bed. Neither Tom nor Saul
can understand a word he says, but Kitty understands. She refuses
to tell who he is because she has promised him to be silent. Tom and
Saul carry him to the farmhouse where he can be nursed properly
and where Saul can keep an eye on the relationship.

Then the father, Nicholas Tear, enters the story. He is a simple
and innocent Manx farmer and lover. Saul's first move had been to
put the stranger under the pump to wash him, but the father comes
with a bowl and a rag "like a woman with a baby" (II, 126). Mrs.
Tear, on the other hand, is a hard, unloving Manx woman who
thinks it not "dacency" to have a tramp in the house. Kitty carries

on conversation with him but neither Tom nor the father, Nicky-Nick-Nick, can understand his Midlands accent.

In the second part of the poem, Tom Baynes returns two years later from a voyage to China. He helps with the harvesting and finds Kitty and the now recovered visitor walking in the moonlight. They call the visitor Ned, and Nick Tear highly approves of him. Nick is pleased to have an excellent servant on the farm for nothing but the keep. Mrs. Tear will have nothing of the love affair, for the young man has no name. When Saul comes home, he too is in a rage about the lack of a name. He accuses Ned of being a thief or a vagabond, but Ned holds to his resolution to remain silent about his name and his past. Ned agrees that he will marry Kitty only when he can use his own name.

Jinny Clague, Kitty's cousin from one of the middle parishes of the island, comes to visit. She is cross-eyed and squinty but Saul pays attention to her, and Jinny falls desperately in love with him. To please Saul, Jinny persuades Kitty to reveal the stranger's name, Edward Blake. As soon as Saul hears, he leaves for Ramsey, the major city on the north of the island, and the police. Since Blake is under indictment as a Chartist, he is apprehended and sent to England for trial. Saul is lost overboard on his very next voyage. Blake, in prison when a prison rebellion begins, saves the governor with his wife and daughter. Blake is pardoned by the Queen, returns to the island, and marries Kitty.

Again, the best parts of the story are lyric moments. With comic exaggeration, Nicky Tear explains to Tom Baynes why Mrs. Tear is fearful of her daughter marrying a man without a name. The harvest and the courting scenes are beautiful genre pictures. Kitty is strong and faithful; her squinty cousin Jinny, the cause of the revelation, is very well done; she is a lively woman but not marriageable. The story can be justified for the picture of Nicholas Tear, the mountain farmer, who is so charmed by his daughter and her suitor. In effect, the reader forgets the creaky plot and attends to the father: the plot exists to put him into action to help his daughter, to challenge his fearful wife, to encourage the lovers. The method allows Tom Baynes to be lyrical about the bare mountain landscape (a new setting) but to pass over the death of Saul in one line.

III *The Teachers*

The third story in *"The Doctor" and Other Poems*, "The School-

Masters,'' is even less a story and more a genre picture than "Kitty
of the Sherragh Vane.'' The narrative is simply a series of pictures.
The love story that seems to be the center of the poem collapses, for
the third schoolmaster is not an ambitious Scots bachelor but a
man with a wife whom he has left behind. When the wife turns up,
the schoolmaster leaves with her, and the Manx girl who had fallen
in love with him is left heartbroken. The story ends. The young
Scotsman has exposed the other two schoolmasters as ineffectual
and cost them their jobs. In addition to the usual vivid scenes, the
story gives Tom Baynes opportunity to consider the schools in
Manx life. There are school scenes in "Tommy Big-Eyes," but this
story concentrates entirely on the life in schools.

The first master is Danny Bewildher. Baynes has forgotten his
real name, for he has taken on the name of his action. Danny never
teaches the children letters:

> "Latthars!" he'd say, "idikkiliss! [ridiculous]
> Just clap a Testament in their fiss,
> And off they go — aw, bless your heart!
> They'll read soon enough, if ye give them a start.
> Latthars! latthars! bewild'rin' the childher" —
> And so they were callin' him Danny Bewildher.   (II, 158)

The children memorized their Testaments and Danny thought they
were reading for him. The second teacher is James Clukish, who is
clerk at the Church and also schoolmaster. His daughter Maggie is
Tom Baynes' age; his son is named Mark. Tom started to school to
Danny Bewildher, but when Tom's mother got into a battle (a bur-
lesque epic) with Danny after Danny punished Tom, he changed to
the church school where Clukish was the master. Tom doesn't learn
much, but he does join the choir with Maggie and Mark and, as
usual, he falls in love with the girl. Mark writes poetry, but he soon
goes off to be a draper. All that we know about Mark's poetry is
that it is sad.

An inspector arrives to check the schools. When he visits Danny
Bewildher, he hears Danny's story about letters and the Testament,
but when the inspector gives the children another book, they can't
read, and so Danny is dismissed. A Scot then comes to take
Danny's place.

> He wasn't shy, [as Manxmen are],
> This Scotchman, at all — aw, 'deed he wasn'

> For the cheek he might have been fuss-cosin
> To Ould Harry himself. Aw, the cock o' that nose
> And the strut, and the lip, and the tasty clothes!
> And snuff and snarl, and snip and snap —
> He was what you'd call a pushin' chap —
> Pushin', bedad! and a new light,
> And come to set us all right,
> That was sittin' in darkness and the shadow of death;
> And his name was Alexander Macbeth.
>
> But the chap was good-lookin' — that's the pint.
> And a tongue in his head like a 'varsal jint.   (II, 164–65)

Not only does Mr. Sandy Macbeth take over Danny Bewildher's school, but he is soon angling to get the principal school at the Church from James Clukish. Clukish is agreeable about retiring from his school; he keeps his job as clerk and he also notices that Macbeth is taking up with his daughter. The parish agrees that the match is splendid, "a chance / That wouldn' often come Maggie's way." The parson said, "Mr. Macbeth is a man of promise, / And a most respectable person, Thomas" (II, 166). Tom doesn't like Mr. Macbeth, but Mark, the brother, and everyone else, does. Even Dr. Bell approves of Macbeth.

Macbeth has high ideas. He is not satisfied that he has both schools in the parish, but now he reads for ordination to become a curate for Parson Gale. The day before his ordination a woman comes down the road crying, "Where's my Sandy? where, or where?" She is Sandy Macbeth's wife whom he had left at St. Bees on the Cumberland coast. She spends the night with Sandy and the next day they leave for England.

The men in the fo'c's'le want to know what happened then to Maggie. Tom says that he saw her not more than a week afterwards "spreadin' clothes on the hedge" and he asked her how she was getting on. She said, "I'm very well. / *Very well! very well!*" but the next day she died, "quite aisy, they said — / *Mirrieu! Mirrieu! dead! dead!*" (II, 171). The "Mirrieu! mirrieu!" is the sound of death that the poet Mark had heard the birds sing.

"Kitty of the Sherragh Vane" and "The Schoolmasters" complement one another. In both, the foreigner comes and, because of his greater efficiency and knowledge, quickly impresses the natives. Edward Blake delights Nicholas Tear because he can read and cipher; he helps in the farm as Sandy Macbeth helps in the schools.

Ned's secret is political as opposed to Macbeth's private secret, but
in both cases the harm is deep. Both of these men, in turn, contrast
with Dr. Bell, a Londoner who has become a native. In all three
stories the Manx are charming but ineffectual.

Brown's method in these *Fo'c's'le Yarns* is both typical of the
nineteenth century and yet independent. In one sense the stories
exist to fill out the character of Tom Baynes. We learn to know him
and to trust his view and therefore trust his vision of Manx life.
Brown successfully completes a circle: the stories create Tom
Baynes but Tom Baynes creates the stories. We "suspend our dis-
belief," in Coleridge's fine phrase, because we believe in Tom
Baynes. The force of his personality or his vision makes the stories
possible. As stories, they are little more than gossip of a small community. Edward Blake, to Tom's great pleasure, finally marries
Kitty Tear. Poor Maggie does not get to marry the ambitious Scots
schoolmaster, but Tom Baynes approves of her dying for her love
just as he approved of Mrs. Cain's suicide in "Tommy Big-Eyes."
Her loveless marriage had caused the terrible mistakes. Out of that
bad marriage, however, comes the final pairing of Nelly Quine and
Tommy Big-Eyes. After the bleak and sterile openings of Brown's
myths, some possibilities for human love to make his Manxmen
and Manxwomen happy emerge.

We can see the evolving mythic desire when we pull back from
the details of these stories to perceive their larger patterns. The
doctor was trapped into a marriage with an ignorant, common
woman who could neither raise his children nor provide him with a
home, but the doctor triumphs because he discovers out of the
disaster his love of and duty to his sick Manxmen. Harriet's son
and the doctor's daughter marry, and thus the story follows the
convention that comedy ends with the birth of a new and better
society. Edward Blake is honest and true and, therefore, according
to Tom Baynes and Nicky Tear, a proper husband for Kitty of the
Sherragh Vane. Maggie Clukish falls in love with the bright,
anxious young Scotsman who reforms two schools and is on his
way toward reforming the church too before his wife reappears.
Maggie dies heartbroken, but her death testifies to an imagined life.
Tom Baynes penetrates into these lives and makes judgments on
them for us. He shows that the ignorant Kelly family are inferior in
blood and judgment; he knows that Harriet and Dr. Bell are fit and
proper lovers. Tom Baynes makes the judgment on Saul's jealous
nature. Tom Baynes is himself in love with Maggie Clukish and

mistrusts the ambitious, energetic Scotsman who fools both Parson Gale and Dr. Bell. What lifts these stories from Manx gossip told by a sentimental Manx sailor is the power of vivid language that Thomas Edward Brown could re-create for the sailor's utterance.

The question of whether Thomas Edward Brown and Tom Baynes are the same is, ultimately, foolish. Tom Baynes is a fully created character. He is created as he is because Thomas Edward Brown was a Manxman and could imitate the speech patterns and syntax of the Manx. It is possible to imagine a living Tom Baynes, but the genuine form would only be repeating lively (and possibly boring) gossip from an obscure community. Because Thomas Edward Brown had read his Homer, the Bible, Shakespeare, Dickens, Browning, and Tennyson, he could change the vivid gossip into stories dramatizing in the free world of art how members of a small, inbred community can learn to incorporate a physician from southern England like Doctor Bell, a radical reformer from the Midlands like Edward Blake, or a smart, pushy Scotsman like Alexander Macbeth. The unions fail. Always, however, the subject is an imagined reality created by Tom Baynes.

> For it isn' every fool that's fit
> To make a rael good lie, that'll sit
> On her keel, and answer her helm — no! no!
> Just try it Bob! Just try it though!
> Well put together! you're took on the sudden?
> You couldn'? Didn't I tell ye ye couldn'?
> Lies! What lies! the things I'm tellin'
> Is the abslit truth — ax Neddy Crellin!
> Ears is ears, and eyes is eyes,
> And fax is fax, and that's the lies! (II, 2)

Who speaks? Tom Baynes or Tom Brown? The language is Baynes' but the thought, as it always is, is Tom Brown's. Baynes is the created voice that can make characters dance in a fictional world where truth is truth and facts make song.

CHAPTER 9

The Larger Aim:
Fo'c's'le Yarns: Third Series

You write as if you lived in fearful places,
So that, at times, your best friends wouldn't swear
You are the steady gentleman you are.
                          "Mary Quayle," II, 279.

IN 1889 Thomas Edward Brown published *The Manx Witch and Other Poems* and thus all but completed his epic of Manx life. The book includes two poems, "The Christening" and "Peggy's Wedding," in Anglo-Manx but not narrated by Baynes. The stories were not printed among the *Yarns* in the *Collected Poems,* their place being taken by "Job the White," a poem first published in 1894. "Job the White" completes the story of "The Manx Witch." Tom Baynes, introducing Job in "The Manx Witch," describes his beauty and promises, "Another night / I'll give you Job... / Aw, a ter'ble story."[1] Thus the final placement of "Job the White" in the series was clearly Brown's own intention.

As usual, Brown was publishing poems written long before. Both "The Christening" and "Peggy's Wedding" were finished in December, 1878. "Mary Quayle, The Curate's Story" is dated November 25, 1878, and "Bella Gorry: The Pazon's Story" is dated June 29, 1880. In a letter of October 18, 1886, Brown said that "The Manx Witch" was taking shape,[2] and he quoted two lines from well into the story. Of the six poems in *The Manx Witch,* only "The Indiaman" is undated. Since Brown's wife died after a long illness in 1888 and since he was busy publishing *The Doctor* in 1887, "The Indiaman" also must have been lying on his desk for some time.

In the same letter that told about "The Manx Witch," Brown reported a visit to the Isle of Man:

146

But it really does seem to me as if the whole Island was quivering and
trembling all over with *stories* — they are like leaves on a tree. The people
are always telling them to one another, and any morning or evening you
hear, whether you like it or not, innumerable anecdotes, sayings, trage-
dies[,] comedies — I wonder whether they lie fearfully. They are a marvel-
lously *narrational* community. And you've not been there a day before all
this closes round you with a quiet familiarity of 'use and custom' which is
most fascinating.[3]

The previous chapter suggests that Tom Baynes' skill with language and character changes the gossip of a small island community into writing of considerable interest. Most of the stories told
on the island were as ephemeral as a daily newspaper. Why should
the community be so interested in story? Since 1830 (the year of
Brown's birth) the Isle of Man Steam Packet Company provided
regular service with England and thus regular contact with another
culture. The thirst for story proves the Manx effort to understand a
new invasion. Communities tell stories not only for amusement but
to seek control over powers in the world. The ancient Greek comedy and tragedy depend upon an ancient ritual of the seasons.
Characters represent spring and winter and by destroying winter or
fostering spring characters the community achieves a control over
its destiny. From common observation we know that traumatic
events in a family — births, weddings, and deaths — produce more
than usual tale-telling and reminiscing. Joseph Campbell said that
the Indians on the American plains, as they saw the buffalo dying
and a whole mode of life disappearing, turned to drugs that in-
duced visions and dreams. From these dreams and the stories based
on them, the Indians painfully restructured an order of life.[4]
Brown, in his twelve Manx stories, was trying to articulate, and
possibly manipulate, powers and forces in Manx life. The island
itself "was quivering and trembling all over with stories" in an
effort to understand and control an unclear destiny. After inva-
sions by Norse, Scots, and English, the Manx faced a new invasion:
the tourist. Brown's stories all turn on the new invasion of British
power. He speaks the myth of undeveloped people. His stories act
out emotions (as he said in a letter) which are too deep for
thought,[5] i.e., too deep for rational analysis.

I *The Curate*

The least successful story in the whole sequence comes out

nakedly to state the need for myth. The story has no resolution,
just as Brown found no resolution to the issue of his identity as a
Manxman. The unsuccessful story, "Mary Quayle: The Curate's
Story," was written at the same time that Brown wrote the two
superb vignettes, "The Christening" and "Peggy's Wedding,"
both in genuine Anglo-Manx.

"Mary Quayle" is told by a curate in the curate's English. He belongs to that new breed that has learned the language of men "by
Heaven ordained with pen / And sword the populous world to
teach" ("Braddan Vicarage," I, 4, 11. 62–63). Standing on one of
the highest mountains on the island, a young Manxman, Richard
Craine, tells the curate that he had once come to this same place
with his sweetheart, Mary Quayle. From the height, the two looked
down on their home village, Maughold. The summer before,
Richard had met a young Englishman, Herbert Dynely, visiting the
island on his holiday from Oxford. Even though Mary Quayle is his
sweetheart, Richard recognizes that in comparison to Dynely he is
but a candle to the sun. Dynely is "a wonder" unmatched by any
native Manxmen. Compared to Richard himself "this Dynely
looked a perfect god — / There's nothing like it since the world
began, / The beauty of a noble Englishman" (II, 278). Mary feels
"wonder" when she feels herself "dear / To such a man"

> so that, when the crest
> Of that great wave of love rose to her breast,
> She floated off her feet, and drifted out
> Into love's deep-sea soundings: no faint doubt
> Was in her mind; through all the depths she clung
> To that strong swimmer's arm; and, as he flung
> Around her all the glory of his youth,
> He seemed to her the very soul of truth.   (II, 278)

The metaphor of the girl feeling the water rise and then finally float
her is the kind of metaphor that Tom Baynes would have used for a
whole apostrophe to love. In "Mary Quayle" the metaphor is
serviceable to the story of Mary's downfall. She allows herself to
float in her love for Dynely, and when Dynely leaves, she knows
that she is pregnant.

Mary's mother tells Richard. The family — her three older
brothers and a Methodist father — takes the news phlegmatically,
make no effort to communicate with Dynely, nor do they seek
revenge on him. Dynely is, to them, "just / A reef that they had

split upon" (II, 281); he is a blow of wind that capsized "The ship in which they'd stored what most they prized" (II, 282). The pregnancy is simply a fact of nature.

As soon as Mary's child is born, Richard sails on the packet for Liverpool; he goes to Dynely Hall to tell the news to Herbert Dynely. Richard is impressed by the size and majesty of the place, and the stately home frightens him. He knows that nothing "Could make it possible for Mary Quayle / To be the mistress there" (284). Richard falls in a swoon and then gets to his knees to pray. The prayer asks what has separated Mary and Herbert. Richard resolves to give her up so that Mary and Herbert can be happy in their love. He falls asleep by a stream knowing that Herbert will come by the spot since it is a fine day for fishing. Herbert awakens Richard from a dream about Mary and her child. When Richard tells Herbert about the child, Herbert asks Richard if he loves Mary (they had never spoken her name the summer before). For an instant Richard wants to revenge himself, but he steels himself to prefer Mary's happiness and denies that he loves her. He does speak harshly about the wrong that is done to Manx girls treated as toys, "slaves of lustful joys / To you, and such as you, that you may break them / For fun and fancy" (II, 287). He asks what God made the moral law, the God of heaven and earth or the "devil-god."

> "God, and law!" I cried;
> "Your God is Moloch, and your law is pride —
> Hell's pride; man's law — man therefore can reverse it —
> Stand up with me, I say, and curse it! curse it!
> Curse it! it is no part of God's great plan —
> *A gentleman!* stand up, and be a man!"   (II, 288)

The speech is effective and Herbert agrees to come to the Isle of Man the following Friday. Richard takes money from Dynely to get home as quickly as possible with his news. On Friday, however, Dynely is not on the boat; on Saturday they read in the paper that he has drowned while fishing. Then Mary dies. She is buried in Dynely Church.

It would not help to know that the story really happened. The story probably occurred repeatedly; it still occurs in undeveloped countries. A young girl born on the Isle of Man has few opportunities. She might well look forward to meeting one of the half million visitors (in Brown's time) who came during the summertime. More than likely Brown simply had no way to end his story. It may be man-made law, even Moloch's law, that divides lovers such as Mary Quale and Herbert Dynely, but to counter that law with the law of chance resolves nothing. The curate, an Oxford man, might recall the ending of one of Matthew Arnold's Marguerite poems which also tells about parted lovers,

> A god, a god, their severance ruled!
> And bade betwixt their shores to be
> The unplumbed, salt, estranging sea.[6]

The lightning metaphor in "Mary Quayle" makes vivid the sheer elemental nature of Manx life. At the beginning of the poem, the curate and Richard watch a storm come to the sea near Maughold Head, the headland where Mary's village is located. The black cloud is "slumb'rous with brazen light." While Richard tells his story, "The lightning leaped" (II, 275).

> "Mary was ruined, sir;
> She bore a child that was not mine —
> Nay, do not stir —
> The lightning, is it? Sir, we may resign
> What's ours, if so we make it happier;
> But oh! to see it in the dust,
> Down-trodden, broken —
> Aye, and by one in whom you had full trust,
> Stained and defiled,
> That is the grief that never can be spoken —   (II, 275–76)

Richard says that Mary is struck by lightning and he asks "Who's angry with the lightning?" (II, 282). When he dreams about Mary at Dynely Hall, Richard sees her child lit by "a ball of rosy flame" (II, 286). By the end of the story, the storm has dissipated and a full moon appears. The curate says that he sees a face in the night sky with a "robe of silver, and ... crown of gold." The good woman dies; the genuine Manx question of how to cope with visiting Englishmen (or with raiding English, for that matter) is still unresolved. It is no more explicable than lightning.

II   *The Fire Lighter and The Seaman*

Two stories in the *Fo'c's'le Yarns: Third Series,* "Job the White" and "The Indiaman," are vignettes. Each, however, contributes another dimension to Brown's theme of love and redemption. "Job" actually completes the story of "The Manx Witch," the first story in the final series, since Job is the witch's son. The Witch is "goin' a spilin' " [spoiled] / In English sarvice, ... / More English till Manx" (II, 251). The Witch has died before the story of "Job the White," but her influence is still felt.

"Job the White" and "The Indiaman" appear in this discussion out of place — the principle of this discussion is chronology of composition — in order to keep "The Manx Witch" for a climactic position in the next section. "Job" and "Indiaman" expand TEB's range in time and in method. In time, they occur almost yesterday (say the 1880s). One story, "Job the White" is a tragic story; the story of life aboard the Indiamen is a rollicking comedy in Brown's best manner. These stories vary TEB's Manx myth, a myth that comes to a focus in "The Manx Witch."

The Manx witch dresses her son, Job, in white when he is a baby, and Job continues to wear white after his mother's death. Tom Baynes believes the white connotes the essential purity and truth in Job's behavior. He is the archetypal (so his name, of course) good man who suffers. In "Job the White," Job is a shepherd and Tom Baynes tells about seeing him like an angel with his flock. Job follows his mother as she goes to fairs and public events to keep her in order. A neighbor, Tom Cowla, makes fun of old Mrs. Banks and Job thrashes him. In return, neighbor Tom shoots the white pigeons that Job raises. When Job is found dead along the road, the whole community judges neighbor Tom the murderer and they are ready to lynch him, but he is whisked off in the nick of time by tram to Douglas.[7]

In addition to shepherding, Job lights the fire at the mouth of the lead mine on Sundays at midnight, for the workers on the Monday morning shift. He is murdered one Sunday night on his way to work by William, another of TEB's thwarted lovers, who had not intended to murder Job at all. Frustrated William had been watching Job's neighbor, a young girl who meets her lover each night. While they are courting,

> all the time
> This 'illiam was burnin' like the lime
> On the slack — not a wink, not a word, not a look:
> Burnin', burnin', and the Divil's crook

Twisted in his innards there.
Jallous! jallous!   (II, 259)

William's frustrated love gets warped as in the cases of Mrs. Bell (the physician's wife), Mrs. Gale, or Cain, the Methodist. Aiming to murder his rival, William mistakenly strikes Job with an ax and kills him. Tom Baynes says it was no blunder. William "knew it was Job the very first blow, / But he couldn't stop" (II, 260). He confesses and he is hung for the murder. Baynes accepts the hanging but argues against some of his audience who deny that a confessing and penitent man may be hung.

This story is also about the inexplicable evil in the world and misdirected love. William is jealous, but from all that the story says, he is an old man who could have no hope of loving the girl. Because he cannot stand the sight of love, he sets out to murder and, instead of the real suitor, he accidentally murders the simple and good man Job. Early in the story Job is compared to Christ; at the trial William says Job is

> "like a sacrifice,
> Like offered up, like Christ, like Christ!
> The Lamb of God, the chosen Prince,
> And me to be off'rin' him up for the sins,
> Oh yes! I thought, for the sins of the world."   (II, 260)

It is, in fact, the very goodness of Job that makes him eligible for the terrible event. There is no explanation for evil; it simply exists in William's poor befuddled mind. Thus TEB moves even further into pure myth of good and evil (recall Melville's *Billy Budd*).

If "Job the White" is a rustic tragedy, the story that follows it, "The Indiaman," is a comedy at sea. Fanny Graeme comes aboard an India-bound ship at Liverpool; she catches her dress on the gangway and falls into the arms of a sailor, Peter Young. The only plot is Tom Baynes' ineffectual efforts to keep them apart. The captain of the ship assigns Baynes to the job. Baynes makes rules about limiting the number of hours they should spend together, limiting the number of kisses, and even limiting their actions, but they always fail to keep the prescribed order. Tom thinks he has played the role of the father successfully and kept the lovers apart, but many years later Tom meets Fanny on the train from Liverpool to London with her eldest son. She had married the sailor.

If evil is inexplicable then so is love. Fanny falls into the arms of a sailor: "A chance, a glance, a touch, a breath, / And there you're lovin' unto death" (II, 264). Tom beats up Young and nearly causes a mutiny in the fo'c's'le when his men suggest that he is behaving like William Cowla, but Peter Young seems to understand Tom.

The stories are short and the whole charm of them lies in Tom Baynes' innocent way of dealing with essential life rhythms and designs. In both stories, accident produces the ending. Blindly and randomly both murder and love occur. Man has no mastery over the force of love — except in his stories. Events strike like the lightning in "Mary Quayle."

III   *The Miners*

"The Manx Witch" is one of Brown's most successful stories. It is subtitled "A Story of the Laxdale Mines" and thus it adds a new occupation to the survey of Manx life. The lead mines at Laxey were one of the few sources of island wealth in the nineteenth century.

Two young miners, Jack Pentreath (his father was Cornish) and Harry Creer seek the hand of Nessy Brew, a farmer's daughter. The whole crew of miners have formed a kind of lodge of courters to ward off the courting drapers and shoemakers from Douglas and even some ship captains so that the miners themselves have a clear field. Finally, Jack persuades the group to retire from the scene and leave the courting to himself and Harry. Harry is a *dooiney-molla.* Manx for "man-praiser," the phrase refers to "the friend who backs, and speaks praisingly of the suitor" (II, 197, n). Harry is more a comic figure than a comic rival.

Jack Pentreath and Nessy court in a "garden of Eden" (II, 203–04), and the devil in this story is the Manx witch, Mrs. Banks, Nessy's aunt. Nessy's father, however, won't have his sister living in his house. Tom Baynes says that she has a pension from the devil (II, 208), but he explains that she had been "in England in a sitchuation, / Lady's maid, or something o' the surt" (II, 233) where she had learned her witchcraft. She becomes — like Edward Blake or Alexander Macbeth — an outsider whom simple Manx people fear.

The situation is perfectly suited for Tom Baynes' favorite subject. He tells the men about love:

> It's the best thing, the best,
> It's the only thing, just the one bright flash
> That quivers through this world of trash
> And make-believe.   (II, 192)

Both Jack and Harry have been struck by the flash, but Jack more. Actually the men would have worked out the problem easily enough if it hadn't been for the witch, who resents the fact that Nessy's father has forced her to live in a small cottage away from the farmhouse. Jack, too, dislikes having the witch in the house while he is courting and finally orders her away from Nessy too. Petrified that Jack might be punished for offending the witch, Nessy tries to excuse Jack's behavior and under pressure gives her mother's wedding ring to Mrs. Banks in return for the witch's promise not to bewitch Jack. Nessy is simple and credulous.

Mrs. Banks keeps her word, but she tells Harry Creer, the *dooiney-molla*, to stop playing his role of mere helper; he should do some courting on his own. When Harry tries, he and Jack argue and decide to fight it out at the mouth of an abandoned lead mine. Tom Baynes, coming home from a wedding, hears them struggling and at first thinks the sound comes from devils. Tom throws water on them to stop the fighting and finally forces them apart. He says, "If you're wantin' a grave, / You'd batthar spake to the Clerk... / And get a comfortabler place / than that" [the mine shaft] (II, 226). Then he advises,

> "And now be quick,
> And on with your clothes!" For the chaps was bare
> To the very buff — aw, 'deed they were!
> And the moonlight shinin' on their skin —
> These naked divils — astonishin'!   (II, 226)

The scene is reminiscent of the wrestling scene in D. H. Lawrence's *Women in Love.* They had fought for over two hours, but only after Tom begins to question them do they discover that the witch set them at odds. They decide on a new strategy with Tom's help. They fire a silver bullet at a rabbit found near the witch's house in the hope that wounding it will lame the witch. It doesn't work. Jack goes back to his courting, and Harry accompanies him to entertain Nessy's father (Harry is a very good spitter). Since Nessy, however, cannot relax and enjoy the courting, Jack feels sure she is still under the influence of the witch. Jack goes to a lawyer for help, but he is thrown out of the office. They then try Parson Gale who assures a doubting Jack Pentreath that the New Testament has rid civilization of witches no matter how much Jack cites Old Testament texts to prove their existence.

The parson also promises to speak to Nessy, to release her from fears of a witch's power, but says, "It's you that gives them the power... / By believin' in all this wickedness" (II, 244). Innocently the parson thus defines the basic discovery of nineteenth-century art and philosophy: the mind creates categories of meaning. Brown overtly states in this poem what he had stated earlier in his English lyric, "Dartmoor." In the second half of that poem, when the creative spirit of the universe speaks, the spirit says "Why, you [man] are Lord, if any one is Lord." Perception makes good and evil. The Manx witch was in simple fact no witch at all, but a woman who had picked up English manners. Jack and Nessy create the devils which so afflict them; they would be Lords of their world if they were not seduced by the witch's English experience and knowledge. What is awkward and forced in "Dartmoor" is natural, direct, and evident in "The Manx Witch."

Again the story succeeds because of the vitality of Tom Baynes' telling. He catches the scene of the miners' courting club, the courting scenes, Jack's talk with the lawyer, and his arguments with Parson Gale that the Bible proves that witches exist. The farm where Nessy lives is a Garden of Eden. When Jack and Tom Baynes talk to the parson, the name of "a blind ould party / By the name o' Milton" (II, 242) is used as part of the argument. He had an eye inside, "an eye that clear / It could split the bottom of darkness in two." Tom does not understand Milton, but his name is used to justify the banishment of witches. The devil in the story is the outsider, Mrs. Banks, who has been contaminated by her experience in England. Her own brother banishes her from his house but cannot keep her out all the time. Although the parson says that witches have their power because men give it to them, Nessy continues to believe.

The reader understands perfectly that the small community cannot tolerate a woman as different as Mrs. Banks is. She has been to England; she dresses in strange, even bizarre costumes. She has a son who is not quite bright; she is given to fairs and gin. When she is first introduced in the story, she seems innocent.

>   Sally Behind —
> The aunt, you know, a widow woman,

And a sister of Brew's, that was imp'rint [impertinent], uncommon,
And bad with the tongue; she was goin' a-callin'
Sally Behind, for the way she was fallin'
Abaft of her midships.   (II, 180)

As the story develops, she becomes in the eyes of the characters
more and more sinister until they are utterly impotent to face the
power they give her. When they cannot understand a behavior, they
attribute its cause to their own invention of the witch's power. The
story makes comedy out of a familiar defense mechanism.

"The Manx Witch" has the ability to sustain comedy on a very
serious subject. The comic tone consistently develops. On the way
home from the fair Jack and Harry, who are pretty well in liquor
themselves, decide to try to kiss Nessy, but she slips out from between them, and when they feel each other's whiskers, they realize
they are kissing each other. Parson Gale hears some of the story
when he offers Nessy a ride home. When she slips away from him,
he worries about her. At dawn he wakes Jemmy Brew, the father, to
ask if Nessy is at home. Jemmy, a tremendous sleeper who never
knows what happens about his farm at night, shouts to wake up his
daughter. She appears at her window just as the first rays of sun
strike the house. The father can't figure out why the parson has
come. Could he have been drunk? Nessy suggests he might have
wanted eggs. Then the father thinks he might have wanted to buy
one of his cows. The reader knows the logic of each character's
behavior, but since the characters in the story do not, each invents
reasons to explain action. Since Brew sleeps so soundly and snores
so loudly, men come from all over the country to court Nessy. Even
Mrs. Banks can come to the house in the evening despite Brew's
orders that she stay away. The miners court happily with Brew
asleep but Mrs. Banks restricts them. The reader sees all. The result
is a beautiful and almost classical farce on a folk theme. The farce
depends on exactly the same theme as "Mary Quayle" — delusion
by a power that is created in the individual's mind — but the farce,
paradoxically, treats the theme with more subtlety and much more
artistry than "Mary Quayle." The story ends, archetypally, with
the marriage of Nessy and Jack: the powers of darkness have been
both created and defeated.

Is Mrs. Banks a witch? She dresses extravagantly and paints her
face, but at no point in the story does she act like a genuine witch.
She teases poor gullible Nessy, and she is shrewd enough in her

judgment of character. When her body is found at the bottom of the lead mine shaft, her hand is rooted into the soil by the herb she had gathered. Possibly Nessy and Jack did not delude themselves. The detail, however, seems to give one more turn of the screw to the story of "The Manx Witch." By just such a detail, Brown shows that the game we have been playing with the powers of evil is not entirely a game.

IV *The Harvest Festival*

"Bella Gorry" is the last of the twelve *Fo'c's'le Yarns*. Since it is dated June 29, 1880, it belongs to that decade of creation when Brown was at his full powers as a writer. "Bella Gorry" is written in English and in decasyllabic blank verse. TEB attempted the form only this once, and this poem is a triumph.

The other stories are often mythopoeic. Nessy Brew and Jack Pentreath might be compared to Andromeda-Perseus figures and Tom Baynes compares them to Adam and Eve. They are clearly the work of a mythographer in the sense that Brown's stories return so frequently to the impotence of the single or isolated Manx spirit. "Bella Gorry" exists in a stranger world than the folk habit of the other story. Bella, a southside woman, is thirty years old when she appears on the northwest coast of the island.[8] She is a harvest worker and only accidentally does the parson find the nest she has made with turf along the sea for her infant child. The story never explains who fathered the child; possibly he was an Englishman. The farm workers build a rustic home for Bella and her child Sarah. Bella supports herself by field work, but she dresses Sarah in fantastic costumes. The parson fears that Sarah will be sent to school in her outlandish garb, but he talks Bella into more restraint. There is some difficulty at Sarah's confirmation because the cap Bella makes seems inappropriate. The parson is sure that he cannot keep the gossips quiet, and so Sarah is confirmed without a cap. A strangeness, however, lingers in everything Bella does.

When she grows up, Sarah, the daughter, is employed by a Liverpool family summering in Ramsey. She returns to Liverpool with the family, but both the parson and Bella fear for her safety in the city: "I have known of many / Caught in the snares of your great Liverpool" (II, 305). That city "pollutes" and "devours" and "to think of it is death!" The city is the Manx hell. In other *Fo'c's'le Yarns* it is spoken of the same way. Jinny Magee, in "Betsy Lee,"

dies in a public house in Liverpool. Tom Baynes describes his unjust arrest in Liverpool (II, 29).

When Sarah comes home, the community turns her visit into a
holiday.

> It was a real little festival
> When she came home to see us: every face
> Was brighter for her look, such interest,
> And such excitement, in the parish here!
> . . .
>
> It came to be a custom of the place;
> And I was always there, and nothing loth —
> Such little things made up our round of life,
> And are the landmarks of its quiet course.   (II, 306)

The parson speaks the justification of all these stories: the stories
become a custom of the place; they make up the round of life and
become its landmarks. The parson takes Sarah on the last steps of
her journey to her mother's house. Bella never comes out to greet
her. She stays in her house, waiting. "It grew to be a custom, as I
said, / A ritual of observance most exact" (II, 307). The return is a
"Sabbath time for Bella" when Sarah brings presents for the children. The detail of the harvest, the unfathered child, the alien
mother, and Sarah's fanciful clothes demand a wider meaning. In
fact, the story resembles the Demeter-Persephone myth. In the
ancient myth the daughter returns from hell and brings with her the
spring and summer season. In 1889 Tennyson published "Demeter
and Persephone," his version of the myth. If Brown is retelling the
myth, the perception is all in his reader's eye and mind.

The final scene of the story varies from any comfortable retelling
of an ancient myth by a simple country parson. After nine years of
returning to the island, Sarah writes to say that this year she will
bring a husband. Bella asks to spend one last night alone with her
daughter, and the husband plans to spend the night at the vicarage.
The parson is pleased with the husband, who was "acquainted /
With much that lay beyond my beat — the arts / Of busy life, and
ways of toiling men" (II, 308). They walk along the beach, but
before they return to the vicarage, they stop to look in the window
of the cottage. Bella has undressed Sarah and, kneeling, kisses her
knees and her breast. The parson describes the scene as a "Sibyl
clinging to this Venus" in an "ecstasy of love" (II, 309).

The next morning the men dress to go to the cottage, and Sarah meets them at the door. She greets them "with a voice that seemed unmoved," but once inside, she turns back the coverlet of the bed, "and there / Lay Bella, with a sunbeam on her brow, / A bright young sunbeam — Bella, sir, was dead" (II, 310). The story offers no explanation. The parson says that the doctors called it heart disease. The final two lines, "Westward to Jurby, eastward, as I said, / The coast runs level to the Point of Ayre" (II, 310), repeat almost exactly the fine controlled majesty of the opening lines of the poem:

> Westward to Jurby, eastward if you look,
> The coast runs level to the Point of Ayre,
> A waste of sand, sea-holly, and wild thyme —
> Wild-thyme and bent. The Mull of Galloway
> Is opposite. Adown the farthest west,
> Not visible now, lie stretched the hills of Morne.
>
> *A cottage,* did you say? Yes, once it was;
> A ruin now.   (II, 295–96)

Thus the poem returns to the bare landscape on the coast where the mysterious event occurred.

"Bella Gorry" is the only story in the sequence that lacks "tragedy ... ruin ... and death" (II, 305). It repeats the cycle of life. Bella is the eternal mother; when Bella dies, her daughter seems not to grieve. The cycle will repeat again, and the poem starts again with the words that began it.

V   *The Completed Cycle*

Thus ends Brown's own cycle of Manx life. The twelve poems are like the twelve months of the year or the twelve signs of the zodiac. The sequence started in Tom Baynes' unsuccessful love; it ends with a fatherless child revealing to her husband the death of her mother. In the cycle the flash, the strike, the moment of human love gives meaning and significance to human affairs. The stories repeat the platitude that "God is love," but in their variation the flat, dull statement once more interests and attracts a reader. The cycle has also ranged through the classes and stations of Manx life in the 1840s and 1850s ("The Manx Witch" and "Job the White" alone seem to occur in the late part of the century). Farmers, sea captains, and miners feel the stroke of love. In the process, the reader witnesses a kaleidoscope of Manx affairs, the customs of the people. The subjects of Brown's English lyrics — alienation, loss of faith, human love — have been incorporated into the stories. His subjects grow out of the actions and the emotions seem more genuine, human, and attractive than in the lyrics.

In the *Collected Poems,* the *Fo'c's'le Yarns* fill five hundred pages, eighty percent of Brown's published work. Even the twenty percent that remains contains "The Christening," "Peggy's Wedding," "Mater Dolorosa," and the sequence of scenes called "In the Coach," all written in Anglo-Manx dialect. "The Christening" is a monologue of exultation spoken by a father in celebration of the birth of his first son. It has the high glee of fulfillment. "Peggy's Wedding" reports, the day after the wedding, the comic events that occurred on the wedding night. Peggy was not allowed to stop at a public house for a drink, and when she arrived at her new husband's house, she found it a ramshackle mess. Further, he had no money and immediately appropriated all of Peggy's savings. Thus Peggy returned to the job she had as a house servant. "Mater Dolorosa" is a woman's speech comforting her husband after the death of their child. "In the Coach" records a sequence one might hear in a diligence going from Douglas to Ramsey. The first story concerns a group of Manx sailors who are invited to enjoy, but too shy to accept hospitality in Scotland. In the second scene a young sailor tells about the sea chest of a Manx sailor who has died in Bombay. In the third scene, titled "Conjergal Rights," a husband, married just the day before, tells why he is on his way to see a lawyer about his rights as a husband. The scene hilariously inverts the situation of "Peggy's Wedding." The fourth scene, "Going to Meet Him," is spoken by a young girl in anticipation of meeting her sweetheart, Billy Sayle, and then she speaks of her disappointment afterwards. At the end of each speech, a chorus of "Conscious women" says "Poor sowl! poor sowl!" The scene is funny, touching, and beautiful. In the fifth scene, "The Parsons," a man who objects to parsons speaks. At the end of his ranting complaint, Parson Gale enters the coach — and suddenly the speaker reverses himself in obsequious deference. The final scene, "Noah's Ark," presents scraps of dialogue between a woman in the coach and new occupants who enter first with a calf and then a donkey. The protesting woman insists that she is not in Noah's Ark. The stories are all lyrics. Because they are shorter than the narratives in *Fo'c's'le Yarns,* these occasionally are included in anthologies. Brown's tact and control is supreme in each one of them, and the innocent outrage is marvelously humorous.

These additional Manx lyrics demonstrate again TEB's ability to create character by speech alone. He continues to choose quite ordinary Manx men and women, but he still achieves wide diversity. The middle-aged narrator of the story about the sailors refusing the invitation in Scotland could be Tom Baynes himself. In other speeches he creates by their own words a sailor, a farmer, and the silly but adorable girl in such anticipation about meeting her sailor-lover. The raucous Methodist who hates parsons recalls Cain in "Tommy Big-Eyes," but this man is all innocent guile and a fool. "Peggy's Wedding" is pure dialogue between the mistress of the house and her servantwoman. In "The Christening," the speaker captains a Manx fishing boat. When these persons are added to the gallery Tom Baynes creates in the *Yarns,* we may fairly conclude that Brown has a Dickensian ability to re-create character. It is all very well to say that he copies directly from nature; the wonder is that he succeeds so well and so convincingly that we seem to catch, in a moment, an entire life and an entire nation. As Tom Baynes says in "The Doctor," it is as hard to tell the lies of fiction as it is to build a trim sailing ship. These Manx lyrics are all neat and tidy like a good sailing ship.

Brown's method is like that of a photographer, especially the photographer who catches in a wrinkle or a tilt of the head some mark of character. His men and women have the same clarity as those in the photographs of the American Civil War by Matthew Brady. Brown's characters appear complete with wrinkles and moles showing. Speech alone creates them; he seldom needs physical detail to define their genuineness. A repeated speech pattern suffices for the Methodist-farmer Cain in "Tommy Big-Eyes." Nicky Tear, the farmer in "Kitty of the Sherragh Vane," eagerly helps his daughter's love affair. Frequently Brown's characters seize us because of their complete love and admiration of others. Tom Baynes falls in love with Betsy Lee, Christmas Rose, and nearly every other woman he meets. Not only are his women such loving creatures, his men — except for an absolute villain like the Methodist Cain — care for one another. Parson Gale seems hardly to live for himself. They are so human and innocent that they attract us as children attract us. The people seem utterly natural, as in a photograph. They are complete — with some particular trait given predominance to amuse us.

The genuine comic hero is a witty rascal who brings the whole world within his power because of his wit, but this comic hero rarely appears in modern comedy. Our heroes are humorous characters. They are caught in some habit of behavior or speech, and they win — if they win — by sheer perseverance. Jack Pentreath, the lead miner who ultimately wins Nessy Brew, does not win the fight at the mine with his rival Harry Creer and thus carry his bride off in triumph. Tom Baynes stops the fight, which neither was winning. Since Brown seldom writes the scene of comic celebration, he concentrates all his attention on the quirks of character and behavior. In ancient comedy, public lies — such as parental order or public laws — stand between the hero and his final marriage to his bride. In Brown's stories, private delusions impede his heroes. When Brown's stories end badly, the reader quickly perceives that they need not have ended so badly if someone had just had a long, sympathetic talk with Anthony Lee or Betsy herself. The Gale boys absurdly loved Christmas Rose. The doctor's wife might not have destroyed her children and her marriage if she had learned to be more comfortable in that marriage. If Richard Craine had only mentioned his interest in Mary Quayle, Dynely might not have seduced her. "The Manx Witch" illustrates this self-delusion. Both the lawyer and the parson tell Jack Pentreath that the witch is a figment of his imagination, but still the lovers are kept from their happiness. Thus the quirk that makes the characters funny is often the same behavior that prevents the final comic victory.

Brown's comedy suits his age. The ability to love unreasonably or the honesty of human feelings interest Brown more than the final triumph of the comedy written by Aristophanes or Molière. The Manx character is hardly triumphant even in the wildest imagination. He inhabits a quiet limit of the universe and his safest defense, like that of other minority groups, is to laugh at his weaknesses and foibles and to cherish them. Rather than let them be lost "in the tide / Of Empire" ("Spes Altera," I, 95), TEB recounts the habits and customs of the Manx. He expects no victory; he creates the Manx life, "the landmarks of its quiet course," and thus gives the stability of festival, order, and design to life.

VI   *The Completed Artist*

After Homer created his epic or Wordsworth his lyrics, later writers try to emulate their success. To do so is natural and right. Once an epic has been written, audiences want the pleasures again, and writers use the audience's expectation for their new purpose. Brown's twelve narrative poems form a Manx epic (really there should be twenty-four stories). They are spoken to a listening audience; they range widely through classes and orders of Manx life. They show the special consciousness that makes Manx speech and the Manx soul. The Manxman, for example, is "just the shy." He is insecure, hesitant, doubtful of his own power. TEB's poems thus run counter to the normal expectation of epic poems where actors larger than life, epic heroes, are capable of great feats of valor to demonstrate the public virtues that their nation must follow. Tom Baynes is no Ulysses nor Parson Gale a Priam. For all his charm, Tom Baynes models no future race. Thus Brown's attempt to write for his people differs strikingly. His characters are much more interested in feelings, sentiments, love; they have no concern to establish a new commonwealth. Of course, Brown differs; he lives in another time with other needs. In the nineteenth century a new reading public wanted to read domestic epics about persons who manage, somehow, to live despite the odds. Surely the charm of Dorothea in *Middlemarch* is that any woman could imagine herself living Dorothea's life. Writers constantly complain that they live in such a rapidly changing time; with such gifts bewildering time, no man of perfect virtue can walk before our sight. The virtues change too rapidly. Tom Baynes — like the men and women in the domestic novels — has feet of clay from the beginning. We then are dazzled by our discovery that their lives have quiet, hidden virtues that we can feel and understand and respond to. We might be Tom Baynes loving every girl he sees, growing rhapsodic over common sights and common events.

Brown's stories created a new Manx consciousness. Tom Baynes lives just as surely as Ulysses, or King Henry, or as the man down the road who tells amusing tales. Tom understands Manx life and its values. He is what he is, an honest product of his time, his soil, and his people. Baynes does not speak the words in Dr. Johnson's *Dictionary,* the words Robert Brown used in his poems. Just as surely as standard English, his indigenous speech and soul show passion and beauty as vividly as the known tradition. Thus the speech, the "use and custom," the ceremony of Manx life become alive. Brown's narratives hold a mirror up to Manx experience to show a nineteenth-century Manx feeling on ancient subjects. Jack

Pentreath loses his Garden of Eden with Nessy Brew; Job the White is cruelly murdered because of folly and sin. Wordsworth predicted such poetry when he wrote the "Preface" to his first collection of poems, *Lyrical Ballads* (1800). He was going to cast the charm of the unusual over the ordinary. Wordsworth's "Preface" is a Declaration of Independence of the modern poet; as a result of that essay, writers put down on paper the thought of ethnic groups or the thoughts of marginal men (Wordsworth wrote about an idiot). Brown could not have written his poems one hundred years before; one hundred years later we find his work a preserved amber of a marvelous world.

By writing in dialect, Brown set himself apart from every Scotsman, Englishman, American, Australian. He sacrificed a large audience to write for the Manx, but his Manx poems surpass his English poems. The English poems grant him insufficient room for wit and lyricism. The Manx narratives, however, open the Manx humor, the lambent flame of human love, and the glow of a landscape. Brown's stories connect the trivia, the gossip, of Manx life with the universal rhythm of human experience. Innocently and directly, they show the mythic or the sacramental in life. They are outward and visible signs of inward and spiritual states. Thus the Manx may continue to try to understand their eternal invaders — Norse, Scots, English, and finally, tourists — who carry pleasure away and leave suffering to the Manx. Tom Baynes' loss of Betsy Lee, the furious anger of Captain Hugh, the struggle of Tommy Big-Eyes against the degenerate Methodist Cain are recognizable Manx events, and the actions gave Brown his opportunity to do what he did best — to sing the joys of childhood by the shore, to describe young lovers in an apple orchard, or to show a Manx farmer who cannot resist helping young lovers to find their happiness (even when he has little himself). Brown's lyric moments in his narratives combine the best of two separate nineteenth-century traditions — each grand enough alone but better in Brown's synthesis: he told stories with the vigor of a novelist and with the joy of a lyric poet.

Oxford University made possible a career in literature that TEB wanted as a young man. Oxford gave John Henry Newman, John Ruskin, and Matthew Arnold a style; Oxford's pressures forced TEB and Lewis Carroll to find new expression. Oxford opened to Brown a larger world than his father's cramped Manx rectory. Oxford wounded TEB when it insulted and isolated him as a Servitor; it introduced him to High Church Anglicanism and made him unfit for a Manx rectory himself. Still the High Churchism made him seek also the deep rhythm of experience to make it outward and visible. Had Oxford succeeded, it would have de-nativized him and made him an Englishman. It succeeded well enough so that TEB became Master of the Modern Side, Clifton College, Bristol, but Brown's real life was the imagined life where the "gorse runs riot in Glen Chass," where the "blaeberries on old Barrule" wait to be picked, or where the lichens at Bradda Head draw the soul ("Clifton," I, 71–72). In his free, imagined world, Tom Baynes re-creates an ale house, an epidemic, or an energetic Scots schoolmaster reforming his school and the church. Like Adam, Brown named Manxmen and their places; like a modern writer, he opened the Manx heart. Few have done more. No Manxman has ever done it so well. Oxford drove him to live secretly and to speak in an almost secret dialect, and for that pain, paradoxically, we must be grateful.

Notes and References

Preface

1. *Poems of T.E. Brown, with an Introductory Memoir by Sir Arthur Quiller-Couch,* 2 vols. (Liverpool, 1952). Reprints poems from *The Collected Poems,* ed. H.F. Brown, H.G. Dakyns, and W.E. Henley (London and New York, 1900). Hereafter cited as *Poems. Letters of Thomas Edward Brown,* ed. Sidney T. Irwin, 4th ed. (Liverpool, 1952), hereafter cited as *Letters.*

2. *Thomas Edward Brown: A Memorial Volume, 1830–1930* (Cambridge, 1930), p. xiv; Quiller-Couch's "Memoir" was first written for this volume.

3. "Life of T.E. Brown: Manxman, Scholar, Poet,"Ramsey [Isle of Man] *Courier,* May 2–July 4, 1930.

4. *Letters,* p. 131.

5. Matthew Arnold, "Preface" to *Essays in Criticism,* in *The Complete Prose Works of Matthew Arnold,* III, *Lectures and Essays in Criticism,* ed. R.H. Super (Ann Arbor, Mich., 1962), p. 290; James Anthony Froude, words about Oxford," *Fraser's Magazine* (March, 1850), reprinted in various editions of Froude's miscellaneous essays and in *Victorian Literature: Prose,* ed. G.B. Tennyson (New York, 1976), pp. 658–63.

6. J.M. Wilson, [Isle of Man] *Times,* May 5, 1930.

7. Epifanio San Juan, "Toward a Definition of Victorian Activism," *Studies in English Literature* 4 (1964), 583–600; "The Question of Values in Victorian Activism," *Personalist* 45 (1964), 41–59.

8. *Letters,* p. 11.

Chapter One

1. Rolfe Humphries, trans. *The Aeneid of Virgil* (New York, 1951), pp. 167–68.

2. William Wordsworth, "Preface" to *Lyrical Ballads,* in *Poems* (London, 1933), p. 937.

3. E.H. Stenning, *Portrait of the Isle of Man,* new ed. (London, 1965), p. 14.

4. R.H. Kinvig, *A History of the Isle of Man* (Liverpool, 1950), p. 31.

5. Stenning, p. 14.

6. Ibid.

7. W. Ralph Hall Caine, *Isle of Man* (London, 1909), pp. 1-2.

8. Kinvig, p. 70.

9. The title page reads: Poems; / Principally / On Sacred Subjects. / By the / Rev. Robert Brown, / Minister of St. Matthew's, Douglas, Isle of Man. / 'If I one soul improve, I have not lived in vain.' / Beatties' Minstrel / Published by James Nisbet, / 21, Berners Street, London, / M.DCCC.XXVI. The book contains an eight-page introduction, 137 pages of text and 15 of notes. The preface is dated Douglas, Isle of Man, February 1826.

10. Wordsworth's lètter is in the Manx Museum.

11. *Poems,* I, xiii; one of the poems "brought him an appreciative letter from Wordsworth with a set of the poet's six-volume edition with an autographed inscription." The six-volume edition, however, was published in 1837.

12. E. de Selincourt, ed., *Journals of Dorothy Wordsworth* (New York, 1941), II, 402; Ernest de Selincourt, *Dorothy Wordsworth: A Biography* (Oxford, 1933), p. 402.

13. *Letters of William and Dorothy Wordsworth: The Later Years,* vol. II: 1831-40, ed. E. de Selincourt (Oxford, 1939), II, 661; Samuel Norris, *Two Men of Manxland* (Douglas, 1948), p. 81.

14. *National Commercial Directory of the Whole of Scotland and the Isle of Man: 1837.* n.p., n.d.

15. Isle of Man *Times,* Apr. 25, 1894.

16. D. Wordsworth, *Journals,* II, 404.

17. Ibid., 405-06.

18. Hugh Stowell Brown, *Autobiography,* Intro. W.S. Caine (London, 1887), p. 3.

19. W. Ralph Hall Caine, *T.E. Brown: The Last Phase of the Poet's Life* (Douglas, 1924).

20. Poems, I, X.

21. D. Wordsworth, *Journals,* II, 416-17.

22. Ibid., 417-18.

23. *Mona's Herald,* Jan. 16, 1895.

24. A.W. Moore, *Manx Worthies, or Biographies of Notable Manx Men and Women* (Douglas, 1901); John Stowell, 1762-1799, wrote satirical poems for the *Manks Mercury.*

25. *Manx Worthies.*

26. J.J. Kneen, *Personal Names of the Isle of Man* (London, 1937), p. 78.

27. "Braddan Vicarage," *Poems,* I, 4-5.

Chapter Two

1. Unpublished letter to Macmillan, Jan. 2, 1893. Brown outlined a

projected book of essays entitled "The Island Diocese." The book was never written.

2. *Poems,* I, xiii, xviii.

3. *Mona's Herald,* Jan. 16, 1895.

4. H[ugh] Stowell Brown, "A Quarter of a Century in the Nonconformist Ministry: A Lexture" (London, 1873), p. 12.

5. *Examiner,* Feb. 1895.

6. "Old John," st. 1, *Poems,* I, 5.

7. Unpublished letter, Feb. 28, 1886; in a letter of May 20, 1850, from Moore to the Provost and Fellows of Worcester College, Moore speaks as a father and guardian of Brown's interest.

8. *Poems,* I, xiii.

9. Samuel Norris, *Two Men of Manxland* (Douglas, 1948), p. 88.

10. "Old John," *Poems,* I, 7, st. 13.

11. *Mona's Herald,* Jan. 16, 1895.

12. *Ramsey Courier,* Jan. 21, 1893.

13. Unpublished letter to his sister Margaret, Jan. 3, 1894.

14. *Poems,* I, xiii.

15. *Mona's Herald,* Jan. 16, 1895; the information is repeated in the "Memoir" and in Norris, *Two Men.*

16. Ibid.

17. Norris, p. 82.

18. Unpublished letter, April 16, 1889; he writes about "the relief, or what you will, . . . his sisters must have felt in getting away from" Kirk Braddan Vicarage.

19. H. Stowell Brown, "A Quarter of a Century," pp. 12–13.

20. Major K.S.S. Henderson (Compiler), *King William's College Register: 1833–1927* (Glasgow, 1928), p. 37; entered August, 1844, left Midsummer, 1846.

21. *Mona's Herald,* Jan. 16, 1895.

22. *King William's Register.*

23. K. Forrest, *Manx Recollections* (London, 1894), pp. 40–41.

24. *Poems,* I, xix.

25. Hugh Stowell Brown, *Autobiography,* Intro. by W.S. Caine (London, 1887), p. 32.

26. Joseph E. Douglas, Manx Museum Mss. 1327 C.

27. "Old John," *Poems,* I, 12.

28. H.F.B[rown] and H.G.D[akyns], eds., *Poems of T.E. Brown* (London, 1930), p. 267; in an unpublished letter, Oct. 10, 1881, TEB reports an illness but also his recovery after a long holiday; "I never go forth upon such expeditions without thinking . . . of men like yourself who go on in the same place, and in the same routine of work from year to year. I envy you this quiet fixity of action and purpose." He also talks about the strain of teaching.

29. Letter, May 13, 1892, part of which is printed in *Letters,* pp. 96–97.

30. *Manx Worthies.*

31. Unpub. letter, Nov. 24, 1848.

32. Unpub. letter, Jan. 24, 1854.

33. Unpub. letter, May 7, 1853.

34. Unpub. letter to Harriet, Jan. 27, 1854.

35. *Letters,* pp. 292–93; TEB wrote just after Moore's death, and the sense of Moore's fatherhood is implicit in the whole letter.

36. Ibid., p. 294.

37. Isle of Man *Examiner,* Apr. 13, 1895; *Poems,* I, x.

38. Unpub. letter, Feb. 10, 1895.

39. *Manx Worthies,* p. 40.

40. In a letter to Margaret, Mar. 14, 1896, Brown reports that such stories did not please the Drury family. The story here is from the *Examiner,* Apr. 13, 1895, TEB's lecture "Old Kirk Braddan and Parson Drury."

41. *Manx Worthies,* pp. 35–36.

Chapter Three

1. Joseph E. Douglas, Manx Museum Mss. 1327C.

2. Selwyn G. Simpson, *Thomas Edward Brown: the Manx Poet: An Appreciation* (London, 1906), p. 10; Simpson's source is probably TEB's surviving sister, Margaret.

3. *Letters,* p. 75.

4. Unpub. letter, Jan. 7, 1893; the opening paragraph of the letter, telling about a photograph of his mother, is not printed in *Memorial Volume,* pp. 192–93, where other sections of the letter are printed.

5. Unpub. letter, Feb. 10, 1895.

6. Ibid.

7. *Memorial Volume,* p. 173.

8. Unpub. letter, Apr. 21, 1851.

9. Unpub. letter, May 28, 1854.

10. W. Ralph Hall Caine, *T.E. Brown: The Last Phase of the Poet's Life* (Douglas, 1924), p. 69.

11. Hugh Stowell Brown, *Autobiography* (London, 1887), p. 3.

12. Ibid., p. 8.

13. Wordsworth, p. 468; the sonnet, sixteen in *Itinerary Poems of 1833,* begins "Why stand we gazing on the sparkling brine, / With wonder smit by its transparency, / And all enraptured of its purity."

14. H.S. Brown, *Autobiography,* p. 4.

15. Unpub. letter, Nov. 13, 1850; part of this letter is published in *Memorial Volume,* p. 174.

16. Unpub. letter, Jan. 26, 1851; part of the letter is published in *Letters,* p. 40. In a section about his stay in Liverpool, TEB said someone "swore he shouldn't come into the house." At the end of the letter a per-

fectly clear sentence reads: "There was such raging and 'bull raggin' upon the part of that worthy individual, that I forgot my black top-coat, the most indispensable garment I possess here." The "worthy individual" was clearly Hugh.

17. W. Ralph Hall Caine, *TEB: The Last Phase*, p. 69.

18. *Letters*, p. 14n.

19. *A Supplement to Allibone's Critical Dictionary*, John Foster Kirk, comp. (Philadelphia, 1899), I, 223.

20. Simpson, p. 94.

21. Unpub. letter, Jan. 7, 1893; other portions of the letter are quoted in *Memorial Volume*, p. 192–93.

22. *Letters*, p. 16, reminiscence of Fowler indicates how tangential King William's College life was to TEB.

23. Frederic William Farrar, *Eric, or Little by Little* (N.Y., 1859), the earliest American edition, based on London second edition.

24. *James M. Wilson: an Autobiography 1836–1931* (London, 1932), p. vii; quoted words may be written by Wilson's son, Arnold T. Wilson.

25. The name of the school is in some doubt. It is sometimes called the Academic School and sometimes the Grammar School.

26. *King William's College Register*, pp. iii–xxii.

27. This story may be apocryphal.

28. Unpub. letter, Feb. 10, 1895; TEB is talking about a lecture on Apr. 4, 1895; "I must not forget to speak of Father's ... deep hatred of Bishops and STRANGERS."

29. Wilson, p. 4.

30. Ibid.

31. Ibid., p. 17.

32. Ibid.

33. Ibid., p. 10.

34. Ibid., p. 7.

35. *Letters*, p. 15.

36. Unpub. letter, Dec. 17, 1853.

37. Both Wilson (pp. 13–14) and Farrar in *Eric* (Chap. IX of Part II) tell the story. Farrar has the boy falling 300 feet; Wilson says he fell 60 feet. There is a memorial to the boy in the Chapel at King William's College.

38. *Letters*, p. 16.

39. Ibid.

40. Unpub. letter, Oct. 22, 1849.

41. *New Review*, 13 (1895), 259.

42. Unpub. letter, Oct. 22, 1849.

43. *Memorial Volume*, p. 175, has the name STOKER, but the letters seem clearly signed Stokes.

Chapter Four

1. *Letters,* p. 18; *Poems,* p. xxi; neither cites a source.

2. *Letters,* p. 22.

3. *Macmillan's* 19 (1868), 49–54; quotations in this and the following paragraph are all from TEB's essay.

4. Simpson, 1906, pp. 201–31.

5. *Memorial Volume,* p. 179.

6. Unpub. letter, Apr. 23, 1854. Part of the letter is published in Irwin, but the editor excluded the section on his illness:

"I am not quite well; although I scarcely worked before the examination at all, yet in the examination my mental labour was intense, and day after day while it lasted my friends saw a manifest change in my appearance. Then came the grand dinner at Oriel to commemorate the event, and congratulate the candidates. This gave the finishing stroke to my disorder. I must have eaten some disguised poison I think; for the whole of yesterday I was in that miserable state that I dare say you remember I suffered so much from last autumn during the Schools examinations.... It will soon, like its predecessors, walk off, and I shall be quite right. The most unfortunate part of the business was that I was to have had a small spread in honour of the event, which of course must be deferred til tomorrow."

7. H.R. Trevor-Roper, *Christ Church Oxford: Official Guidebook to the College* (Oxford, 1950); all information on the college is from this source.

8. John Ruskin, *Complete Works,* ed. E. T. Cook and Alexander Wedderburn, vol. 35 (London, 1908),

9. *Macmillan's* 19, 54.

10. Unpub. letter to J.C. Moore, May 12, 1851.

11. Ruskin, I, Chap. II.

12. E.J. Martin, "Thomas Edward Brown," *Church Quarterly Review* 217 (1929), 119–32.

13. Unpub. letter, May 12, 1855; italics added.

14. Unpub. letter, Nov. 4, 1851; he mentions his pimples again in an Apr. 4, 1853 letter, *Memorial Volume,* pp. 178–79.

15. Unpub. letter to Rev. William Kelly, Curate at Sulby, Feb. 21, 1853. The letter is extremely formal although Kelly was his friend. The letter in the Manx Museum is a copy.

16. Unpub. letter, Nov. 7, 1852.

17. Unpub. letter, Apr. 21, 1851.

18. *Memorial Volume,* p. 178.

19. Unpub. letter, Nov. 30, 1853.

20. *Manx Worthies,* p. 110.

21. *Letters,* p. 293.

22. Unpub. letters to Moore, July 16, 1850 and Nov. 6, 1850; the subject of the Tractarians does not appear in later letters.

23. Unpub. letter, Nov. 4, 1851.

24. Simpson; this is the thesis of Simpson's book.

25. *Mona's Herald,* May 7, 1930.

26. Unpub. letter to Kelly, Curate at Sulby, Feb. 21, 1853; several quotations in the next pages are from the same letter.

27. Unpub. letter, Dec. 17, 1853.

28. Unpub. letter, Jan. 27, 1854.

29. David Newsome, *The Wilberforces and Henry Manning: The Parting of Friends* (Cambridge, Mass., 1966), passim.

30. Unpub. letter, June 10, 1855.

31. *Macmillan's* 19, 53.

32. *Letters,* p. 19.

33. *Letters,* p. 21.

34. O.F. Christie, *A History of Clifton College, 1860–1934* (Bristol, 1935), p. 42.

35. Ibid.

36. *Macmillan's* 19, 50.

37. Unpub. letter, Apr. 21, 1851.

38. *Memorial Volume,* p. 175.

39. Unpub. section of letter, Nov. 4, 1851.

40. *Cliftonian* 8 (July 1884), 268–69; the periodical is in the Clifton College Library. *Cliftonian* 12 (July, 1890), 250, speaks of TEB's "earnest championship of one form of ritual, the ancient conventions of manners and letters."

41. William Cubbon, *Thomas Edward Brown ... A Bibliography,* p. 4.

42. Ibid., p. 5.

43. Nowell-Smith, *Book Collector,* 11, 341.

44. Unpub. letter to Margaret, Oct. 27, 1878.

45. Unpub. letter, May 16, 1855.

Chapter Five

1. *Letters,* p. 181.

2. Ibid., p. 20.

3. Unpub. letter, June 10, 1855.

4. *Manx Worthies,* p. 110. In an unpublished letter to Joseph C. Moore, Dec. 17, 1853, TEB writes, "All my friends here (I do not mean junior men) agree in holding that my attainments (as they are pleased to call them) are altogether beyond the requirements of the Isle of Man." He confesses that he doesn't know what to do, but he does announce he will stand for the Oriel Fellowship. In this same letter he says that the night after he won his Double First was the most miserable in his life.

5. Unpub. letter to his mother, June 10, 1855.

6. Ibid.

7. Ibid.

8. Ibid.

9. *Manx Worthies,* p. 110; *Poems,* p. xxvi. The story is also in the obituary notice of the *Ramsey Church Magazine* 2 (Nov., 1897), 200.

10. *Letters,* p. 53.

11. Flaxney Stowell, *Castletown: A Hundred Years Ago,* Intro. by Rev. Canon Kewley (Douglas, n.d.); Kewley's introduction is dated 1902; Kewley offered TEB a room at Oxford in 1849.

12. Ramsey *Courier,* Jan. 21, 1893.

13. Ibid.

14. [Isle of Man] *Examiner,* Nov. 23, 1895.

15. Frederic W. Farrar, *Eric, Or, Little by Little, A Tale of Roslyn School,* Intro. by John Rowe Townsend (London, 1971), pp. 9–10; I have also used the American edition (N.Y., 1859) which differs from the new edition.

16. *Poems,* I, xxviii.

17. (New York, 1859), p. viii.

18. *Eric* (1971), p. 85.

19. Ibid., p. 86.

20. James M. Wilson, *Autobiography,* pp. 7–17.

21. Phyllis Grosskurth, *The Woeful Victorian: A Biography of John Addington Symonds* (N.Y., 1965), pp. 32–41; at Harrow Farrar served under the Headmaster Charles John Vaughan who was forced to resign in 1859 after his sexual advances toward a student became known. Symonds knew about Vaughan's love affair in January, 1858.

22. Roland Austin, *The Crypt School of Gloucester: Established as a Free Grammar School and First Known as Christ School: 1539–1939* (Gloucester, 1939) for the general history; J.H.E. Crees, *Gloucester 1911–1919: A Record of the Progress of the Crypt School* (Gloucester, 1920), p. 25.

23. "Minute Book of the Crypt School, 1860–1880," manuscript in Gloucester Public Library.

24. "T.E. Brown," *The Cryptian,* April, 1913, pp. 36–39. Author says Brown met Naylor at KWC in 1856.

25. All information from the "Minute Book."

26. *Gloucestershire Chronicle.* Quoted from issue of August 31, 1861, when the whole sequence of letters is republished with editorial comment.

27. Unpub. letter, May 28, 1854.

28. *Memorial Volume,* p. 176 (May 11, 1862).

29. O.F. Christie, *Clifton School Days (1879–1885)* (London, 1930), p. ix.

30. O.F. Christie, *A History of Clifton College, 1860–1934* (Bristol, 1935), p. 30.

31. Christie, *Clifton School Days,* p. 12.

32. *Letters,* pp. 20–21.

33. *Letters,* pp. 21-22.

34. Christie, *Clifton School Days,* p. 16.

35. Ibid.

36. Ibid., p. 22.

37. Ibid., p. 27.

38. Ibid., p. 31.

39. Christie, *A History,* pp. 34–35.

40. Ibid.

41. Ibid., pp. 37–38.

42. John Rickards Mozley, *Clifton Memories* (Bristol, n.d.), frontispiece.

43. Christie, *A History,* p. 35; TEB's poem "Old John" was published in 1881, the year after Percival left Clifton.

44. Grosskurth, 32–41; Symonds' father helped found Clifton; Symonds spent time at the school, especially as an adult.

45. *Letters,* p. 203.

46. Christie, *A History,* p. 96.

47. Ibid., p. 39.

48. *Poems,* p. xxxvi. This story is Q's first original contribution to the "Memoir."

49. Unpub. letter, Oct. 10, 1881.

50. W. Ralph Hall Caine, *T.E. Brown: The Last Phase of the Poet's Life* (Douglas, 1924), p. 59.

51. *Crockford's Clerical Directory* (London, 1885).

52. *Cliftonian,* file in college library, Clifton College.

53. Unpub. letter, Oct. 13, 1891.

54. *Poems,* I, 71–72. In 1869 the second line read, "My feet for six long years have trod." Brown erred about Wordsworth's castle, which is actually on the coast of England. There is a Peel Castle also on the west coast of the Isle of Man.

Chapter Six

1. *Poems,* II, 325; subsequent references in text.

2. For dating poems I use Cubbons, *Bibliography;* the "Advertisement" signed by Hugh Graham Dakyns, and the notes in *Selected Poems of T.E. Brown,* ed. by H.F. Brown and H.G. Dakyns (London, 1908); and *Memorial Volume.*

3. *Prose Works of Matthew Arnold,* ed. R.H. Super (Ann Arbor, Mich., 1965), V, 411.

4. *Poems of Matthew Arnold,* ed. Kenneth Allott (N.Y., 1965), p. 105.

5. I use Dakyn's text in *Selected Poems,* p. 281.

6. Samuel Norris, *Two Men,* p. 131.

7. *Selected Poems,* p. 271; I believe the letter was written to Dakyns.

8. Donald J. Gray, ed. *Victorian Literature: Poetry* (N.Y., 1976), p. 883; see also Gray's "The Uses of Victorian Laughter," *Victorian Studies* 10 (1966), 145–76.

9. Nowell-Smith, *Book Collector,* 11, 342.

10. *Selected Poems,* pp. 269–70.

11. *Selected Poems,* p. 279; in *Poems,* the text is "Illustrate or obscure the glory of thy charms."

12. *Selected Poems,* pp. 279–80; *Poems,* II, 371, has "O Heaven! the mannikin!" in the first line, the third line reads "A complex game?"; the fifth line is "The stuff upon thee."

13. *Selected Poems,* pp. vii–viii.

14. William Wordsworth, "Elegiac Stanzas," ll. 14–16, *Poems,* p. 578.

15. Raymond E. Mizer, "A Critical Survey of the Poetry of Thomas Edward Brown (1830–1897)," Unpub. diss. Ohio State, 1952, p. 179; Selwyn Simpson, H.F. Brown, H.G. Dakyns, Lascelles Abercrombie, F.S. Boas, and most of the authors of essays in *Memorial Volume* prefer the English poems. H.F. Brown and Dakyns reprint every English poem in their "Selected" poems.

Chapter Seven

1. E.M.W. Tillyard, *The English Epic and Its Background* (New York, 1954), p. 11.

2. *Poems,* I, 96; subsequent references inserted in text.

3. *Tommy Big-Eyes* (Douglas, n.d.), p. 2; in *Poems* II, 1, the dedication is dated 1887; first published in 1870s.

4. Tillyard, pp. 2–3; Tillyard cites Milton's "Reason of Church Government," Columbia edition, iii, i, 236.

5. "Betsy Lee: a Fo'c's'le Yarn" (Cockermouth, [1871 or 1872].)

6. *The Letters of John Addington Symonds,* eds. Herbert M. Schueller and Robert L. Peters, vol. II: *1869–1884* (Detroit, 1968), 118.

7. *Letters to Macmillan,* ed. Simon Nowell-Smith (London, 1967), pp. 182–83.

8. Ibid., p. 184.

9. Cubbon, *Thomas Edward Brown . . . A Bibliography,* p. 17.

10. Selwyn G. Simpson, *Thomas Edward Brown: the Manx Poet: An Appreciation* (London, 1906), chapter 8.

11. "Christmas Rose" (Cockermouth, 1873), p. 7.

12. Cubbon, p. 16; in the copy in the University of Illinois Library, the preface is dated Nov. 19, 1877, but the date at the end of the text is 1873. Simon Nowell-Smith (*Book Collector,* 11, 343) dates it later.

13. *Letters to Macmillan,* pp. 183, 184–85.

14. Ibid., p. 14.

15. Symonds, *Letters,* II, 120.

16. "Hig-ee Foast (She'll be Comin' Yet)," Isle of Man *Times,* Apr. 6, 1897.

17. *Letters,* pp. 128, 130.

18. Tillyard, p. 8.

Chapter Eight

1. Robert Langbaum, *The Poetry of Experience: The Dramatic Monologue in Modern Literary Tradition* (New York, 1963).

2. Patricia Ball, *The Central Self: A Study in Romantic and Victorian Imagination* (London, 1968).

3. "Dedication: Second Series," *Fo'c's'le Yarns,* in *Poems,* II, 1.

4. *Letters,* pp. 64–65.

5. *Letters to Macmillan,* pp. 183–84.

6. See Dorothy A. King, "Functions of Digression in the Narrative Poetry of T.E. Brown," Unpub. diss., St. John's University, 1969. King did not see the first printings of the *Yarns* where the digressions are even more digressive.

Chapter Nine

1. *Poems,* II, 212.

2. *Letters,* p. 78.

3. Ibid.

4. Joseph Campbell, in a lecture, University of Pittsburgh, 1969; see also his *Hero with a Thousand Faces* (New York, 1968); and his four-*Mythology* (New York, 1962), *Occidental Mythology* (1964), *Creative Mythology* (N.Y., 1968).

5. Unpub. letter to Margaret, May 13, 1892.

6. *Poems of Matthew Arnold*, Ed. Kenneth Allott (New York, 1965), p. 125, lines 22–24.

7. This detail of taking Tom Cowla to Douglas on the tram places the time of the story in the 1890s when the tram was built.

8. Bella Gorry's name recalls King Gorry (or Orrey), an eleventh-century Norse king during the short period of genuine Manx independence. His grave is a landmark on the island; the tram from Ramsey to Douglas passes very near to it.

Selected Bibliography

PRIMARY SOURCES

A. Bibliographies

Cubbon, William, Comp. *Thomas Edward Brown, The Manx Poet (1830–1897), A Bibliography.* Douglas: Manx Museum and Ancient Monuments Trustees, 1934.

Nowell-Smith, Simon. "Some Uncollected Authors XXXIII: Thomas Edward Brown, 1830–1897." *Book Collector* 11 (1962), 338–44.

B. Texts (in order of first publication; I omit sermons, reviews, lectures, and hymns which are listed in Cubbon)

The Student's Guide to the School of "Litterae Fictitiae." Oxford: J. Vincent; London: Whittaker and Co., [1855].

"Betsy Lee: a Fo'c's'le Yarn." Cockermouth: I. Evening, (1871 or 1872).

"Christmas Rose." Cockermouth: I. Evening, [1873].

"The Doctor." Douglas: James Brown and Son, 1876.

"Captain Tom and Captain Hugh: A Manx Story in Verse." Douglas: James Brown and Son, [1878].

"Tommy Big-Eyes." Douglas: James Brown and Son, [1880].

"Old John." Douglas: J. Brown and Son, [1881].

Fo'c's'le Yarns, including Betsy Lee, and Other Poems. London: Macmillan, 1881.

The Doctor and Other Poems. London: Swan Sonnenschein, Lowrey and Co., 1887.

The Manx Witch and Other Poems. London: Macmillan, 1889.

Old John and Other Poems. London: Macmillan, 1893.

The Collected Poems of T.E. Brown. Ed. prepared by H. F. Brown, H. G. Dakyns, and W. E. Henley. London: Macmillan, 1900.

The Letters of Thomas Edward Brown. Ed. by and with an Introductory Memoir by Sidney T. Irwin. Westminster: Archibald Constable, 1900. 2 vols. 4th Ed. Liverpool: University Press of Liverpool, 1952.

Poems of T. E. Brown. Selected and Arranged, with an Introduction and Notes by H.F. B[rown] and H. G. D[akyns]. Golden Treasury Series. London: Macmillan, 1908.

Poems of T.E. Brown. With an Introductory Memoir by Sir Arthur Quiller-Couch. 2 vols. Liverpool: University Press of Liverpool, 1952.

SECONDARY SOURCES

A. Biographical Sources

ANON. (Signed, A Present Cryptian) "T. E. Brown." *The Cryptian.* April, 1913, pp. 36-9.

BROWN, HUGH STOWELL (1823-1886). *Autobiography.* Into. with Notes by W. S. Caine. London: Routledge, 1887.

BROWN, HUGH STOWELL. "A Quarter of a Century in the Nonconformist Ministry: A Lecture." London: Yates and Alexander, 1876. He shows that his life as a nonconformist was better than his father's life in the Established Church.

BROWN, T. E. "Christ Church Servitors in 1852: By One of Them." *Macmillan's Magazine,* 19 (Nov. 1868), 49-54. Signed "Beta."

BUCKLEY, JEROME HAMILTON. *W. E. Henley: A Study in the 'Counter-Decadence' of the 'Nineties.* Princeton University Press, 1945.

CAINE, W. R. H. "T. E. Brown: The Last Phase." Douglas, [1924]. The British Museum catalogs the item under Brown. It is pp. 57-72 of *The Lure of the West Country,* no editor, no further publication data given.

CHRISTIE, C. F. *Clifton School Days (1870-1885).* London: Shaylor, 1930. Christie writes about his student days.

CHRISTIE, C. F. *A History of Clifton College 1860-1934.* Bristol: J. W. Arrowsmith, 1935. A fuller account; he does not repeat information from his first book.

FARRAR, FREDERIC WILLIAM. *Eric: Or Little by Little, A Tale of Roslyn School.* New York: Rudd & Carlton, 1859. A novel set at King William's College; Farrar was a classmate of Brown's. The New York edition is based on the second London edition with its Preface in which Farrar denies that King William's offered anything more than setting.

FORREST, KATHERINE A. *Manx Recollections: Memorials of Eleanor Elliott.* London: Nesbit, 1894. The biography of a pious, evangelical Manx lady. She was a friend of Rev. Drury, the vicar of Kirk Braddan who succeeded Robert Brown.

GROSSKURTH, PHYLLIS. *The Woeful Victorian: A Biography of John Addington Symonds.* New York: Holt, Rinehart and Winston, 1965. Symonds's father was one of the founders of Clifton College and Symonds himself had a close connection to the college and to Brown's friend, H. G. Dakyns. The study offers a quite different perspective on the same subject as C. F. Christie.

HENDERSON, MAJOR K. S. S. (Comp.). *King William's College Register: 1833-1927.* Glasgow: Jackson, Wylie, and Co., 1928.

MARTIN, E. J. "Thomas Edward Brown," *Church Quarterly Rev.* 217 (1929), 119-32.

Thomas Edward Brown: A Memorial Volume. 1830-1930. Cambridge: at the University Press on behalf of The Isle of Man Centenary Committee, 1930. Usually identified as *Memorial Volume.* It includes, in addition to the Quiller-Couch/Radcliffe "Memoir," eleven other essays of "Personal Recollections and Impressions by various friends." It also prints thirty pages of unpublished letters and Brown's contributions to the Clifton College Hymn Book. The Bibliography, by Radcliffe, is superseded by William Cubbon, op. cit.

"Minute Book of the Crypt School, 1860–1880." Manuscript copy of the record of the trustees' meetings, in the Gloucester Public Library.

MOORE, ARTHUR W. *Manx Worthies.* Douglas: S. K. Broadbent, 1901. Both a dictionary of national biography and a Protestant's saints' lives. Moore had seen TEB's letters to Archdeacon Joseph Christian Moore. Especially useful for seeing the influence on Manx life of the fifteen sons of his grandfather's sister, Anne Brown, who married a Stowell.

MOZLEY, JOHN RICKARDS. *Clifton Memories.* Bristol: J. W. Arrowsmith, [1927]. Mozley was the son of Jemima Newman, sister to John Henry Cardinal Newman. Mozley was a fellow master at Clifton.

NEWBOLT, SIR FRANCIS G. *Clifton College Twenty-five Years Ago: The Diary of a Fag.* London: F. E. Robinson, 1904. The diary that Newbolt kept in 1879 printed in one type with his comments and recollections printed in a different type.

NORRIS, SAMUEL. *Two Men of Manxland: Hall Caine, T. E. Brown.* 3rd ed. Douglas: Norris Modern Press, 1948. First Edition, 1947. A crotchety book written by an amateur. Norris prefers Brown. Caine's novel, *The Manxman,* was the first book to sell over a million copies in Britian. Caine says that he has many letters from Brown, but he refused to permit publication because Brown said things too flattering to Caine's work. Norris suggests that Caine stole plots from Brown, but since Caine stole plots from everyone, the theft is no great surprise. The Hall Caine heirs ignored my request for information.

NOWELL-SMITH, SIMON (ed.). *Letters to Macmillan.* London: Macmillan, 1967. Brown's letters on the Macmillan bowdlerization.

QUINE, REV. CANON JOHN. "T. E. Brown," *Mona's Herald,* 7 May 1930. I believe this fine essay was written for the *Memorial Volume.* Quine is too angular and sharp for a pleasant book of reminiscences. Brown helped Quine publish his Manx novel, *The Captain of the Parish* (London: Heinemann, 1897). In his letters TEB talks about how difficult and unbending Quine was as a man. The article may be found in a volume of press clippings in the Manx Museum Library.

RADCLIFFE, WILLIAM. "Life of T.E. Brown: Manxman, Scholar, Poet." *Ramsey Courier,* May 2, 9, 16, 23, 30; June 6, 13, 20, 27; July 4, 1930. The text is nearly identical to that published in the *Memorial Volume* under the name Sir Arthur Quiller-Couch.

SCHUELLER, HERBERT M. and ROBERT L. PETERS (eds.). *The Letters of John Addington Symonds.* 3 vols. Detroit: Wayne State University Press, 1967-1969.

DESELINCOURT, ERNEST, ed. *The Journals of Dorothy Wordsworth.* 2 vols. New York: Macmillan, 1941. See "The Journal of a Tour of the Isle of Man, 1928," II, 401-19.

STOWELL, FLAXNEY. *Castletown: A Hundred Years Ago.* Intro. by Rev. Canon Kewley. Douglas, n.d. Published about the turn of the century. Kewley is probably the friend who gave Brown a room at St. Edmund's Hall, Oxford, in October, 1849, when Brown was admitted to Christ Church.

TARVER, J. C. "T. E. Brown: Manxman, Scholar, Poet." *Nineteenth Century and After* 88 (Dec. 1920), 1020-25. A fellow master at Clifton.

[WILSON, JAMES M.] *James M. Wilson: An Autobiography 1836-1931.* London: Sidgwick & Jackson, 1932. The Preface is signed A.T.W. and J.S.W. The one is Arnold T. Wilson, who was killed in a fighter plane during the Battle of Britain; he was born when his father was Headmaster at Clifton College. The younger son, J.S.W., wrote the connective narrative between the separate autobiographical essays.

B. Unpublished Critical Studies

KING, DOROTHY A. "Functions of Digression in the Narrative Poetry of T.E. Brown." Unpub. diss., St. John's University, 1969.

KOPETZKY-RECHTPERG, HEDWIG. "TEB und seine *Fo'c's'le Yarns.*" Unpub. Diss., Vienna, 1929.

MIZER, RAYMOND E. "A Critical Survey of the Poetry of Thomas Edward Brown (1830-1897)." Unpub. diss., Ohio State, 1953.

SIMPSON, SELWYN G. "Thomas Edward Brown, le poete de l'isle de Man." Unpub. diss., Lille, 1906. See book listed below.

C. Published Critical Studies (Cubbon lists a great many titles, but most are simply book reviews.)

ABERCROMBIE, LASCELLES. "T.E. Brown." *Nineteenth Century and After* 107 (May 1930), 716-28.

BOAS, F.S. "T.E. Brown." In *The Eighteen-Eighties,* ed. Walter de la Mare. Cambridge University Press, 1930. pp. 44-68.

COSTAIN, REV. A. J. "The Manx Poems." In *Memorial Volume,* pp. 151-67. Cambridge University Press, 1930. The only essay in the volume with effective critical judgment.

RIDLEY, M. R. "A Forgotten Poet." In *Second Thoughts,* pp. 133-45. London: J.M. Dent, 1965.

SIMPSON, SELWYN G. *Thomas Edward Brown: the Manx Poet: An Appreciation.* London: Walter Scott Pub. Co., 1906. Canon James M. Wilson's sour introduction begins, "A full and final appreciation of

T.E. Brown as a poet has, in my judgment, still to be written."Simpson prints six early poems and works out a comparison between "Betsy Lee" and Tennyson's "Enoch Arden" to prove that Brown writes a better rural idyll than Tennyson. He attempts to define Brown's attitude toward God.

WEYGANDT, CORNELIUS. *The Time of Tennyson: English Victorian Poetry as it Affected America,* pp. 309–316. Port Washington, N.Y.: Kennikat, 1968 (orig. pub. 1936). "Brown, if you allow that narrative poetry admits to the company of the great, you must call all but major." Although he praises the Manx stories for being Chaucerian in their own way, he regrets that Brown wrote no more English lyrics.

D. Sources on Manx Life

CAINE, W. RALPH HALL. *Isle of Man.* London: Adam and Charles Blake, 1909. Since Brown is a part of Manx history, some of the best comment on his poetry appears in such books as this and others listed here.

KINVIG, R. H. *A History of the Isle of Man.* Published under the Auspices of Tynwald by the Manx Museum and Ancient Monuments Trustees. Liverpool: University Press of Liverpool, 1950.

KNEEN, J. J. *Personal Names of the Isle of Man.* London: Oxford University Press (for Manx Museum and Ancient Monuments Trustees), 1937.

STENNING, CANON E. H. *Isle of Man.* London: Robert Hale, 1950. Of Stenning's two books, this is considered the better.

STENNING, CANON E. H. *Portrait of the Isle of Man.* New ed. London: Robert Hale, 1965.

E. Other Sources Consulted

ALTICK, RICHARD. *The English Common Reader.* Chicago: University of Chicago Press, 1957.

BALL, PATRICIA. *The Central Self: A Study in Romantic and Victorian Imagination.* London: Athlone Press of University of London, 1968.

Crockford's Clerical Directory for 1885. 17th issue. London, 1885.

LANGBAUM, ROBERT. *The Poetry of Experience.* New York: Norton, 1963.

DESELINCOURT, ERNEST. *Dorothy Wordsworth: A Biography.* Oxford: Clarendon Press, 1933.

DESELINCOURT, ERNEST, ED. *Letters of William and Dorothy Wordsworth: the Later Years.* 2 vols. Oxford: Clarendon Press, 1939.

TILLYARD, E. M. W. *The English Epic and Its Background.* New York: Oxford University Press, 1954.

Index